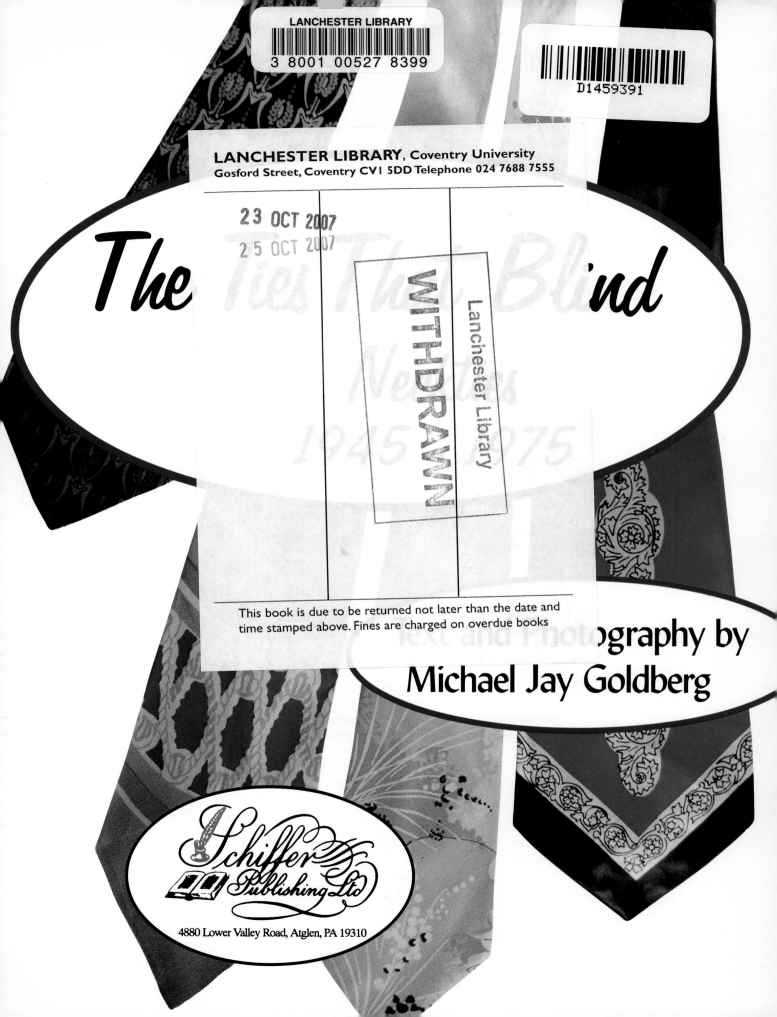

The Ties That Blind

Neckties 1945 1975

Text and Photography by
Michael Jay Goldberg

Schiffer Publishing Ltd

4880 Lower Valley Road, Atglen, PA 19310

Coventry University

Goldberg, Michael J. (Michael Jay)
    The ties that blind : neckties 1945-1975 / text and
photography by Michael Jay Goldberg.
        p. cm.
    Includes bibliographical references.
    ISBN 0-88740-982-2 (paper)
    1. Neckties--Collectors and collecting--United States-
-Catalogs.
    I. Title.
NK4890.N43G66   1997
391.4'1--dc21   97-15392
                                        CIP

"Wembley," "Wemblon," and "Wemco" are registered
trademarks of Wemco, Inc.

Printed in Hong Kong
ISBN: 0-88740-982-2   1 2 3 4

Book Design by Blair R.C. Loughrey

Published by Schiffer Publishing Ltd.
4880 Lower Valley Road
Atglen, PA 19310
Phone: (610) 593-1777; Fax: (610) 593-2002
E-mail: schifferbk@aol.com
Please write for a free catalog.
This book may be purchased from the publisher.

Please include $3.95 for shipping.
Try your bookstore first.

We are interested in hearing from authors
with book ideas on related subjects.

Contents

Acknowledgements

I would like to thank Gerald Andersen of the Neckwear Association of America, New York, for all his kind help and invaluable information and Jim Sutherland for his support and editing skills.

Individuals who loaned or donated ties include: Jim Sutherland, Joan Baggett, David King, John Luccia, and Gaia Hannan, and Mary Alice Cheesman, all from Portland, Oregon; Michael Minckler from Bend, Oregon; Ken Conley from Mechanicsburg, Pennsylvania; Dennis Wanken from Moraga, California; Sue Bartz from Baltimore, Maryland; Kenan Marlin from New Orleans, Louisiana; and Ray Casebeer from Tillamook, Oregon.

John Luccia from Portland and Dennis Teepe from Baltimore, Maryland loaned or donated research materials.

I would like to individually thank the following shop owners for allowing me to photograph ties from their shops as well as their private collections:

Andrea Woodworth of Avant Garden, Portland, Oregon, who can be reached by e-mail at "ruckus teleport.com"

Huan Vu of Vintage ReVu - A Vintage Fashion Clothier, 232 Ankeny, Portland, OR 97204, (503) 241-1876, which offers vintage casual to couture fashions for men and women, including suits and coats, and a large inventory of neckties for men and fashion accessories for women.

Paul Bassett of Avalon Antiques - Vintage Clothing, 318 SW 9th Avenue, Portland, OR 97205, (503) 224-7156, which has the distinction of being the oldest continously running vintage clothes shop on the West Coast. This store features antique and vintage clothing up to 1970, and supplies costuming services for movies, commercials and bands.

Jason Brown and Andrea Crawford of Pokerface - A Retro and Subcultural Clothing Boutique, 128 NE 28th Avenue Portland, OR 97232, (503) 231-4366. Swing clothing, rock-a-billy and mod is how the owners describe the merchandise at Pokerface. The hippest clothing from the '40s, '50s, and '60s are their specialties.

David Donovan of The Bowery of Antiques and Collectibles, 1709 Fleet Street, Baltimore, MD 21231, (410) 276-7577). This collective has a bit of everything, unlike the vintage clothing stores. David was kind enough to let me photograph the tie mock-ups and other items he had purchased from a tie manufacturer.

Preface

Reading the Labels

The captions accompanying the photos in this book contain information derived from the one or more labels sewn onto the backs of ties. It is easy to decipher them with the following information:

Manufacturer's Label - the label for the company that made the tie. Besides the recognizable company name, look for catchwords on the label like "Made in " or "imported from." This label might also indicate a line by the manufacturer with its own name (e.g. Deluxe by Penney's). These labels sometimes have information about fabric as well.

Retail Label - the label that gives the name of the shop and cities where tie outlets were located (such as University Men's Shop, Grand Forks, North Dakota).

Fabric - Many labels indicate the fabric from which the ties were made, found on the manufacturer's label or a little tag attached to the manufacturer's label or elsewhere on the tie.

Registration numbers - In 1939, the Wool Products Labeling (WPL) Act was passed to better regulate the wool and fabric industries. It provided for the registration of products and the assignment of WPL and RN (Registration Numbers) numbers which are found on may labels. These numbers can be of help to the tie collector for identifying companies and manufacturers. There is a directory of these numbers - check with your local library.

Design Titles - as seen on Bold Look, handpainted, and designer ties of the 1940s and 1950s, these are titles of the artwork on the front and are actually screen printed along with the front design on the back of the tie. Countess Mara employed this device frequently, but generally titling artwork was not a popular practice. "Handpainted" is sometimes found printed on ties.

Unmarked - You will also find ties with no labels: these could be homemade or the labels may have come off. The stitching which held the sewn label on older ties tends to unravel with age. I have indicated ties with no labels as *unmarked*.

It was not an easy decision, but I have chosen to not feature certain types of collectible ties in this book. These ties appeal to the specialized collector and frankly, some are quite esoteric and not easy to locate. They include: cowboy and bolla ties, fraternal ties (unions, lodges, etc), school ties, commemorative ties, political ties and ties with traditional designs (with some exceptions). Except for the traditional designs, these have particular strong appeal to historians and historical collectors.

Another kind of ties not represented here, but nevertheless very popular (and also hard to find), are advertising ties. These usually featured a company's trademark, logo, or mascot. They were, presumedly, worn by salesmen and reps or given away as promotions. They don't surface very frequently, but recently I have seen a vintage Pepsi Cola tie with the Pepsi Elf, an International Harvester tie with a tractor and the company's logo, and a Wholsum Bread tie with a loaf of bread painted on the front.

Also absent are ties employing licensed characters, which are enjoying a tremendous boom in contemporary times. I believe all these above-mentioned "excluded" tie categories are worthy of a thorough study and books of their own.

With few exceptions, foreign-made ties are not discussed here except for a few that appear in the Seventies and Eighties sections.

I apologize here for any inadvertent inaccuracies and invite you to contact me through the publisher.

Enjoy these vintage ties! Desire, acquire, admire, and by all means wear them. Who would have thought that a necktie would become such an individual form of self-expression? - But is it art?

Michael Jay Goldberg
Portland
March, 1997

Introduction

Like a belt, it doesn't hold anything up; nor does it, like a shoe lace, hold anything on; it doesn't even hold anything down, as a collar pin does. It has no pockets, and therefore nothing can be carried in it. It doesn't keep a man warm in winter or cool in summer and it won't keep the rain off him. Yet this thing is so much part of a man's clothing that without it he feels at most times almost naked. (Sam Doal, "The Ties that Blind," *New York Times Magazine*, September 11, 1949.)

That part of clothing is the necktie. And when the necktie ran head-on into the twentieth century, neither would be the same. In the last fifty years, the neckwear industry has provided men with an unlimited choice of ties. For it is in these last fifty years that the once-utilitarian necktie has become a means of expression for most men who wear them (and women, too.)

Let's face it - life can be dull! Except for those rare, unconventional types, the majority of us face a routine world when we wake up each day. In an effort to mitigate the effects of this basic truism, we embellish our lives with items that brighten our space, entertain us, and inform us. We choose carefully, if not always knowingly, our wallpaper patterns, our car color, the paperback on the magazine rack, and most importantly our fashions. We base our clothing choices on personal appeal as well as their uplifting quality. The closer the object comes to our physical being, the more likely we are to be particular about how it looks - how it expresses our individuality. Fashion would nicely take precedent in this category. A quick scan through the history of women's fashions gives us lots of information on the evolution of personal expression; women are more apt to be encouraged to "express themselves" through their clothing. Scan men's fashions, on the other hand, and - well, hmmm - not much.

Then there's the necktie. Suddenly things really heat up. The necktie has been one of the only ways the average man can express himself through his clothing on a daily basis. The use of the necktie as deliberate expression is a recent phenomenon. The tie, as we know it today, has moved from utilitarian to self expression in less than a hundred years. Some decry the tie as dead, in a purely social concept, but less than 50 years ago men were *supposed* to wear a tie almost every time they left the house - and sometimes in the house as well. Today, neckties are no longer compulsory with everyday wear, but are still considered part of a man's business attire. However, the somber solid- colored or traditionally patterned "business" ties of yore have been joined by many colorful and interesting alternatives.

Today a man can wear a tie when he *wants* to, and when he *has* to he can choose more freely. The different styles of popular men's ties have followed cycles similar to other fashions. In ties, this cycle usually fluctuates between conservative and traditional styles and bold, colorful and experimental designs. In the last fifty years, artists and designers have created wild, weird, and fascinating tie designs. These periods and the ties that sprang from them are featured in this book. Of the thousands of tie styles and patterns that have been created, we will concentrate on the more eye-catching, artistic, unusual, and sometimes most typical ties of the respective eras.

Ties and Collecting

One of the biggest assets of collecting ties is the large selection of vintage ties available to choose from. Consider the large number of tie manufacturers, both large companies and independent studios, operating during the last 60 years. Of all the ties inspected for this project, each collection contained totally different ties! Vintage clothing stores from Oregon to New York produced a tremendous array of incredible designs. Availability, the bane of other collectibles, is definitely on the side of ties. In the case of specialty ties though, the volume of readily available designs drops dramatically; these ties are the most desirable and in some cases were not produced in large quantities.

Ties shown here are grouped by the time periods in which they were made. With some practice, you can usually date a tie by its shape, fabric, and design. Labels are also helpful, and they will be discussed with the ties on which they appear. The many ties without labels were grouped by their similarities to labeled ties based on their fabric, style, and design. Since many contemporary ties are fashioned closely after older ties and have no label, they can be extremely difficult to identify. Also, new styles do not appear at specific times, so the dating of some is ambiguous.

Retro vs. Vintage

As used in this book, the terms *retro* and *vintage* convey very different meanings. Retro is defined in *Webster's Dictionary* as "backward." The idea of reaching backward into the past seems retro. I use "retro" to define an object from a recent period that was designed and made to resemble an object from an earlier period. In the fashion industry, the "retro look" refers to styles that harken back to the past for inspiration.

Vintage is defined in *Webster's Dictionary* as "the type or kind current or popular at a particular time of the past." I use "vintage" to define <u>actual objects</u> from the past. Therefore, a modern tie made and designed to look like a tie from a past style or era would be a "retro" tie. A "vintage" tie would be an old one. However, when you wear vintage clothes, the act of wearing them would be considered retro. Think about it.

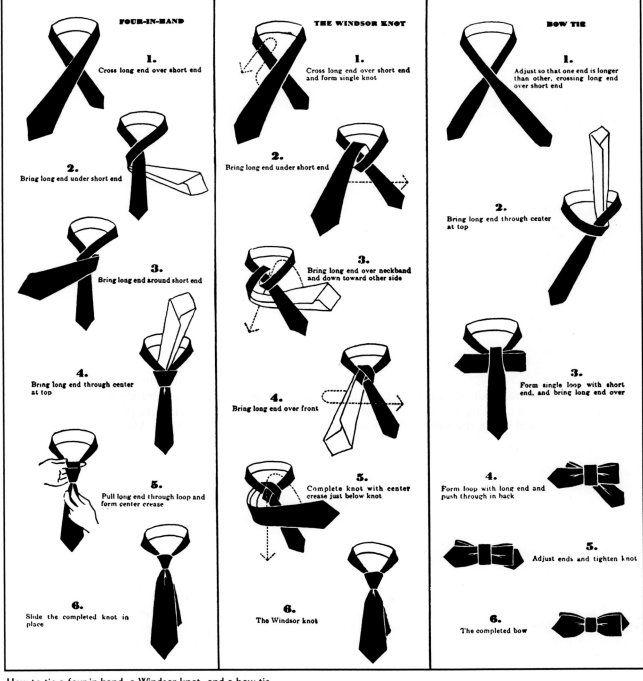

How to tie a four-in-hand, a Windsor knot, and a bow tie.
From *Esquire*, June 1943.

1. The Fabrics of Ties

Fabrics have a mystique of their own. The introduction and gradual development of semi-synthetic, synthetic, and new fibers and the fabrics they created parallel the development of neckties over the last fifty years. In that time, the fabrics of popular ties have developed from natural fibers to semi-synthetic fibers to synthetics and back to naturals again! Along this path are many blends which are combinations of different fibers, be they natural or not. While some ties have the fabric name printed on the label, many do not. It is useful to "get a feel" for the fabrics by doing just that - feel them! Blends can be misleading and synthetics can cleverly mock natural fibers. Regardless of how adept you get at tie identification by touch, the following information about the fibers and the fabrics created from them is useful to know.

Silk

The silk industry started in China and almost all silk in the United States is imported. Silk is universally accepted as a luxury fiber. The International Silk Association of the United States emphasizes the uniqueness of silk by its slogan "Only Silk is Silk." Silk has a unique combination of properties not possessed by any other fiber: a "dry" tactile touch, natural luster, good moisture absorption, excellent suppleness and draping qualities, and high strength.

The beauty of silk and its high cost are probably responsible for the man-made fiber industry. In the early days, before the 1920s, there was no scarcity of natural fibers and thus no need to try to duplicate them. Being a solid fiber, silk was fairly easy to synthesize in a laboratory.

Care: Dry cleaning is usually recommended for silk articles or carefully hand washing in warm water with soap detergent. Do not use bleach. Silk is sensitive to sunlight, which causes white silk to yellow and all silk to break down and lose strength. Silk fabrics are damaged by perspiration.

McCurrach Ties from *Esquire*, July 1944. These silk "corahs" are printed in traditional "British India" designs and seem to herald the arrival of the Bold *Look*.

Floral - : marked Styled by Creveling of California; Forstmann's Charmeen by Superba, 100% wool, painted by hand; Croydon Cravats, all silk.

Wool

Wool, the fur from sheep, and was one of the first fibers to be spun into yarns and woven into cloth. In recent years, wool's share of the cloth market in the United States has steadily declined due to the influx of imported fabrics, competition from synthetic fibers, and the added expense of manufacturers to meet new anti-pollution standards. Wool processing plants rank high as river polluters and so many have been forced to close. Some people now consider wool a luxury fiber, even though wool fabric still is abundant. However, wool fabric is not as readily available as it once was; the cost to make it has risen and the cost to care for wool clothing has discouraged many from owning it, they may prefer the easier care of wash-and-wear clothing.

In the 1960s, when man-made and synthetic fibers were used in increasing amounts, wool was promoted as "nature's wonder fiber" by the Wool Bureau. "Wonder fiber" is an apt description for wool since it has a combination of properties that are unequaled by any man-made or synthetic fiber: namely, its ability to be shaped by heat and moisture, ability to absorb moisture in vapor form without feeling wet, comfortable warmth in cold weather, initial water repellency, feltability and flame retardance. Wool does not soil readily. Grease and oils do not spot wool fabrics as readily as they do other fibers.

Care: Dry cleaning is preferable for wool or hand washing gently in warm or cool water. Wool shrinks in hot water. Do not use bleach. When ironing, use medium temperature with steam. Moths like wool, but chemical moth-proofing is now available.

Cotton

Plants in which strong fibers can be readily separated from the materials surrounding them provide textile fibers, and cotton is the most widely used of the natural cellulose fibers. Cotton has a combination of desirable properties including durability, low cost, easy washability and comfort. This unique combination of properties has made cotton a standard fabric for many of the world's people who live in warm and subtropical climates. Though man-made and synthetic fibers have encroached on the cotton industry in recent time, cotton still remains highly popular and 65% of the fiber in fabric blends is cotton. Soft and sheer batistes, fine muslins, sturdy denims and corduroys all are examples of cotton's widespread use.

Cotton cloth was used in ancient civilizations. The United States did not enter the world market for cotton until 1800. Cotton was grown in the southern states as soon as colonies were established there. Until Eli Whitney invented the cotton gin in 1793, cotton fibers were separated from their surrounding materials by hand. The cotton industry in America was greatly affected when the plantation system of raising cotton was dismantled after 1865 when the Civil War ended.

Care: Cotton is resistant to organic solvents so that it can be safely dry cleaned. It can easily be home laundered in hot water and ironed on high temperature. Cotton should be totally dried before being stored to prevent mildew from affecting damp fibers.

Rayon

Rayon is a man-made cellulose fiber in which the starting material, wood pulp or cotton linters, is physically changed. Rayon was the first man-made fiber and was developed by scientists trying to create artificial silk. Commercial production of rayon in the United States started in 1911. The fiber was sold as "artificial silk" until the name "rayon" was adopted in 1924. The first uses of rayon were for clothing, and its first success was in crepe and linen-like fabrics. Sharkskin, tweed, and chiffon were other forms made from early rayon fibers.

Allover pattern- marked Hand-picked fashions, Rayon; marked Towncraft Cravats; unmarked.

The physical properties of rayon remained the same until 1940 when high-tenacity rayon for automobile tires was developed. Soon after, 65% of the rayon produced went into industrial and household uses. In 1955, a technological breakthrough in rayon production occurred with the creation of high performance (HP) rayon, also known as polynosic rayon. This modified fiber made it possible for rayon to be used for washable fabrics. HP rayon stimulated a resurgence in the use of rayon for apparel. In the late 1950s, twelve companies in the United States were producing rayon.

The rayon used for neckties is usually of the lustrous type. It has a beautiful, silk-like feel and appearance. Since the lus-ter, fiber, length, and diameter of rayon fiber can be controlled, rayon can also be made into cotton-like, linen-like, wool-like, and silk-like fabrics. As a blending fiber, rayon can be given many of the same physical characteristics as the other fibers in a blend. Rayon/silk blends resemble real silk.

Care: Rayon and HP rayon both can be safely dry-cleaned or laundered at home in warm water and ironed on high temperature. Both types of rayon are susceptible to attacked by silverfish and mildew so should be kept dry.

Acetate

Acetate was the second man-made fiber produced in the United States (after rayon). First developed in Europe, acetate's first successful use was as varnish for airplane wings during World War I. After the war, the process of making acetate fibers was perfected and acetate exhibited better properties than rayon for use in silk-like fabrics. It had natural body, which made it also good for blends with rayon for wool-like fabrics. Acetate was first produced in the United States in 1924.

Stitched Brocade - marked Towncraft Cravats; marked Arrow; marked Berkeley (Berkeley ties the world). All three ties are 100% Acetate.

Because acetate was the first synthetic heat-sensitive fiber, consumers were confronted with fabrics that melted under a hot iron. Homemakers of the time were accustomed to washing and ironing all their apparel, and to make matters worse acetate was touted as a new type of rayon, causing consumers to assume they shared the same properties. Another initial problem with acetate was fume fading - a condition in which certain dyes changed color as a result of atmospheric fumes. This problem was not corrected until the early 1950s when a new form of dye was developed and in 1955 triacetate, a new form of acetate, was introduced. Like HP rayon, triacetate was more durable than its predecessor.

Acetate fabrics have a luxurious feel and appearance as well as excellent drapability. It has therefore been promoted as the beauty fiber. Acetate is widely used for satins, brocades, and taffetas in which the luster and body of the fabric are more important than durability or ease of care. Acetate also keeps a good white color, an advantages over silk which yellows easily.

Care: Acetate should be dry-cleaned and triacetate can be either dry-cleaned or machine washed and ironed at a medium temperature. A warm or hot iron will scorch or melt acetate.

Nylon

Nylon was the first *synthetic* fiber and the first man-made fiber conceived in the United Sates. The discovery of nylon was not planned, but resulted from a fundamental research program in polymers at the du Pont Chemical Company in Wilmington, Delaware, in the early 1930s, to extend basic knowledge of the way in which small molecules are united to form giant molecules. By 1939, du Pont was making nylon 6.6 and introduced it to the public in women's hosiery where it was an instant success. The term "nylon" had no special meaning but it had a nice sound like rayon. At this time there were no laws specifying generic names for fibers. Acetate then was still considered a type of rayon.

Nylon was called the "miracle fiber" for several years and had a combination of properties unlike any natural or man-made fiber in use in the 1940s. It was stronger and more resistant to abrasion than any other fiber, it had excellent elasticity, and it could be heat-set. Nylon's high strength, light weight, and resistance to sea water made it suitable for ropes, cords, sails, and the like. As nylon entered the apparel market, its disadvantages became apparent. It had high static build-up causing it to cling and to gather lint. It was not comfortable next to the skin, and had low resistance to sunlight. Early nylon shirts and blouses were said to feel like a film worn around the body. Fortunately, as each problem appeared more was learned about the fibers and ways were found to overcome the disadvantages.

Mention should be made of Qiana Nylon. Qiana is not a modified nylon but is a different kind of nylon made up of unique molecular units similar to those of regular nylon. Qiana is the most silk-like of the man-made fibers. It is soft, supple, and as lively as silk, but with the ease-of-care properties of polyester. The name Qiana (pronounced Key-ah'-na) is du Pont's trade name for fibers that met test standards; the name was chosen by a computer. Experimental fabrics were woven with Quiana fibers by small European weavers and the fabrics were made into dresses by top French and Italian designers in the 1960s. By 1968, the apparel world at large learned about this wonderous new fabric. Though initially an expensive luxury fabric, Qiana began commercial production of more affordable items by 1972.

Care: It is recommended that nylon and Quiana nylon both be dry-cleaned. Like most synthetics, nylon is heat sensitive and should be ironed carefully on a low iron. Nylon is resistant to moths and mildew.

Polyester

When du Pont Company chemists discovered nylon as a by-product of their polymer research project in the 1930s (see nylon section), they discontinued efforts on the general research project in favor of concentrating on the development of nylon. Research on polymers continued elsewhere, and the first polyester fiber, Terylene, was produced in England. In 1946, the du Pont Company purchased the exclusive right to produce polyester in the United States. The du Pont Company polyester fiber was given the name Dacron® (a name that is commonly mispronounced; the correct way is "day-kron") and it was first produced commercially in 1953. In 1958, Kodel®, a different type of polyester, was introduced by the photographic film making Eastman Kodak Company. Polyester's popularity continued to climb. In 1960, there were four companies producing polyester; in 1980 there were 23 producers.

Polyester is the most widely used fiber today. It has been referred to as a "work horse" fiber and "big mixer" because it can be blended with so many other fibers. It contributes its good properties to the blend without destroying the desirable properties of the other fibers. The polyesters (now there are many) have probably undergone more research and developmental work than any other fiber. The polymer is "endlessly engineerable" and many physical and chemical variations are possible. Polyester can be made to imitate satin, cotton, nylon, and even fur!

Care: Dry-cleaning is recommended but polyester can be laundered in warm to hot water. Despite their durable reputation, all synthetics are heat-sensitive, so ironing must be done on a low temperature.

Acrylic

Acrylontrile, the substance from which acrylic fibers are made and from which the generic name is derived, was first made in Germany in 1893. The du Pont Company developed an acrylic fiber in 1944 and started commercial production in 1950 with the trade name Orlon®. Three other United States companies also began to produce acrylics: Monsanto introduced Acrilan® in 1952, Dow Chemical introduced Zefran® in 1958, and American Cyanimid introduced Creslan®, also in 1958. Acrylic fibers are soft, warm, light in weight, and resilient and they make easy-care fabrics.

Care: Acrylic fabrics require middle-of-the-road care; wash and dry at warm temperatures and iron on medium heat.

Caring for tie fabrics

Cleaning instructions for each fabric is provided in the sections above, in case you choose to home-launder your ties. Many tie fanciers and experts in the neckwear industry recommend having all ties **dry cleaned** as a rule, particularly silks and older fabrics.

Stains

The bane of any necktie is not a loud design, but stains. Stains not only damage the tie but reduces its collectible value. Most stains on ties are probably from food, since the tie is placed perfectly on a man's chest to catch any type of food that falls from his mouth. There are two types of food stains: grease such as butter or oil, which can be treated with cleaning fluid, and non-grease, such as juice or tea, which will usually come out with water. Combination stains occur, requiring both processes. Difficult problems should be taken to a dry cleaner.

If you must turn to the experts, you could try Tiecrafters which has existed since 1952 to clean or repair any stained or damaged ties you send them. They also disseminate information about ties and send out guides to buying and caring for them from 252 W. 29th St., New York, New York 10001, or by e-mail at http://tieclean.com

Ironing Ties

In professional tie circles, ironing ties is considered *verboten* because the edges of ties are rolled, and not creased (go look for yourself). The rolled edges contribute to the "body" of the tie and ironing flattens the edges into creases. If you must iron, you should know that all modern irons have temperature settings for various fabrics and they should be consulted; lightly ironing at those temperatures is fairly foolproof. Steam is fine for all of the tie fabrics. Vintage irons may only have low, medium and high settings; follow the care instructions given in the fabrics sections above.

2. Neck-ties before 1945

Since ancient times, men have been wrapping various types of fabric around their necks, mostly for protection. This seemed to go unobserved until 1660. At about that time, the country of Turkey, waging a fierce war against Austria, was defeated. One of the victorious fighting regiments was from Croatia, then a province of Austria. The regiment was soon invited to Paris, at request of Louis XIV, and they arrived wearing brightly colored scarfs wrapped round their necks, tied in the front. This, of course, set off a fashion craze, spearheaded by Louis himself, for the cravat (from the French *cravate*, meaning Croat). Caravat-mania spread so quickly that the first cravats arrived at the American Colonies in less than a year! The cravat continued in popularity for the next two centuries, constantly being redesigned and redefined according to social and political changes.

By 1900, the necktie had been refined into various modes that resemble the neckwear of modern times. One style, however, would survive to become the necktie we have today. Evolving from the post-Civil War string ties in America, that necktie is called the four-in-hand. The name is credited to many origins; it is said to resemble the knot used by a coach driver to control the reins on a four-horse team. Another claim for the origin is a popular social club in London where the latest fashions were to be seen. It is also said the four-in-hand refers to the invisible numeral 4 one draws while tying this style of tie. Whatever the origin, this tie resembles our contemporary ties in length, shape and width. Early

four-in-hands had very narrow widths, but eventually it blossomed out.

During the first decade of the twentieth century, neckties were called "neck scarfs" or simply "scarfs." By 1912, catalogs and sales material were listing neckwear as "ties" instead of "scarfs." This trend continued and by 1920 the word "necktie" generally meant some variation of the four-in-hand. The 1920s ushered in a new decade for neckties. The important invention of resilient construction in 1920, where the fabric was cut on a bias and sewn in segments, made ties more tieable and less prone to tearing and wrinkling. The 1920s also saw greater use of silks, knits and other exotic fabrics. Gold and silver silk ties and wool and silk blends with a textural weave which gave them a three-dimensional look were some of the new items appearing at this time. Color became more prevalent. Solid ties in colors never used before, like hues of green and purple, were being offered. Conservative patterns were becoming more accepted for men's daywear. Evening wear still dictated formal ties in black or white, though the all black tie was starting to lose favor for daywear. A booming economy in America and the frenzied pace of the jazz age created more spending dollars and a new affluent (or at least comfortable) class of men. People wanted new and exciting fashions and were occasionally willing to take a chance by breaking from convention.

The transition into the 1930s would have gone unnoticed had it not been

Wembley Ties from Life, December 1942. Traditional designs still held sway at the beginning of the war years.

14

Wembley Ties from *Esquire*, March 1944. "Insignia Red" and other military-inspired colors were patriotic selling points for merchandisers.

Regal "Royal-Aire" plaid from *Esquire*, March 1944. Khaki and black for men in the service.

for the Great Depression in America. A somber mood trickled down to fashion, including neckties. Men became less concerned with colorful ties and so tie styles remained somewhat conservative through most of the early decade. It's not that colorful ties weren't around - they were - but the demand for them was not as great as in the twenties; "practical" ties became the norm. Advice on choosing a man's tie, from the *Woman's Home Companion* in 1934, offered these practical thoughts:

Small, repeated patterns or any one of the many varieties of checks - not plaids! - are apt to be the best choice for the inexperienced buyer. They are always in good taste and may be worn anywhere. Stripes are risky, although occasionally good. If you must buy them, look out that you don't select a pattern that will turn your husband into a member of the Royal Garrison Artillery. On the whole, it is the way of discretion to leave them alone. And never buy one of the large splashy patterns so dear to the hearts of misguided maiden aunts and *never* under any circumstances select a necktie of watered silk of the variety known as moire.

As with many of the arts during this time period, fashion in America was greatly influenced by European styles. This became no more evident than the interest in British fashion, known for its restraint, which offered simple, stylish, and decidedly conservative clothing for men. The conservative look

was typified by the Duke of Windsor, whose traditional taste in neckwear and his own particular version of knotting his tie (the Windsor Knot) was copied by all classes of American men. British imports were also available and European clothing was considered the best in the world.

The European dominance of fashion ended in the 1940s after the outbreak of World War II. Not only were all exports from Europe stopped, but Americans were plunged into the production of war-related items. Estranged for the first time from European dictums, America was forced to use its own ingenuity and Americans are known to be ingenious. Unfortunately, most of the ties made during the war years were rather

Glow in the Dark "Victory Tie" from West magazine, May 1945, described as offering "protection in blackouts, for its light can be seen at a distance". This novelty tie is a classic collectible for tie enthusiasts and World War Two historians alike.

uninteresting. Interesting color and design existed only in limited quantity. An article in Colliers Magazine of September, 1940, suggests that Americans were finally "getting it," (style?) though

The fact that seventy-five per cent of all ties sold in America are bought by women seems to prove (a) that men are dopes, (b) that men are lazy and can't be bothered, or (c) that women have better taste. Looking back at the period when this latter canard was launched, it seems plain that the great ambition of the men of that generation was to look like a pallbearer. The ladies decided to introduce color into the stupid lives of their mates and, boy, did they introduce it!

This sentiment showed that despite the war, tie concepts were about to change again.

Not all problems with the tie industry were foreign born. Silk, wool, and cotton - as almost all fabrics - were being rationed in America. The disappearance of silk heralded the popularity of rayon, the new semi-synthetic fabric, which could mimic silk's luster and sheen. Rayon was closely followed in popularity and time by acetate, and the stellar careers of these two man-made fabrics skyrocketed in the silk-less 1940s. Another victim of rationed materials was the widths of ties -

not too narrow but definitely not material-wasting wide. With war work as top priority, tie manufacturing slowed to a crawl, increasing the scarcity of new ties. The scarcity created a home movement of women who did their own sewing and this trend resulted in a large number of homemade ties during the war years.

Taste in tie design moved into a new conservatism, not only due to the military influence on fashion, but also the need for conformity in a "let's pull together and win this war!" attitude. Military inspired colors were common, as shown in the Wembley tie advertisement from 1944 offering ties in "Insignia Red" to match the color of certain fighting division logos. Neckties sporting "campaign colors" inspired by American Service Ribbons appeared in Esquire in 1943. These colors boasted names like "Middle East maroon", "Far East green", "Africa brown", "Pacific blue", and "Asiatic gold." Military stripes were also popular, particularly if the advertisement referred to them as "regimental" striping. Traditional designs also held sway. Checks and plaids proliferated and paisleys appeared in various forms.

The first part of the 1940s is not seen as a vibrant time culturally, for the war years, though considered drab, can be viewed as a sort of calm before the storm. This was true for many areas of American life - and for neckties.

3. For-ties Bold

The Bold Look in ties occurred between 1945 and 1952, though these dates, like most, are arbitrary. As with many styles, the Bold Look evolved over a period of time, reached a peak (around 1948) and slowly declined until a new style became preferred. Some of the stronger reasons for the Bold Look's evolution into a full fledged style are suggested here:

The Bold Look was most certainly a reaction to the previous drab and conservative style influenced by the war years. Returning servicemen and homefront workers, tired of conscripted uniforms and war-factory overalls, yearned for bright and happy images. Though the country was going through a tremendous change, optimism ran high. In those times, these ties really did cheer people up.

Signet Ties "Circus" patterns from *Holiday*, May 1947.

Pulitzer ties from *Esquire*, December 1947.

Many of the returning servicemen were young, and these ties were marketed to them with great success. Also, the emerging collective force known as "teenagers" (now acquiring an identity as an age group) found favor with the Bold Look. Their desire for novelty and exuberance and their potential buying power made the Bold Look even more popular.

Tie manufacturers and designers, devoid of European influences during the war, began designing ties based on what materials they had on hand and what Americans wanted. Volume production increased along with better technology. When silk and other imports became available again, along with rayon and acetate, these lustrous materials were very much in demand.

Women began purchasing ties for men in increasing numbers. American women had donned workclothes and gone into the wartime workforce in great numbers. There they were able to gain experience and earn a good salary. Women learned the power that money and experience at a job could hold. When the men returned home, more women were equipped to make decisions as consumers. In the postwar years, 80% of ties sold were purchased by women and most of the top tie designers of that time were women.

Wembley Ties from *Esquire*, July 1948.

Botany ties from *Esquire*, December 1947. Ties in traditional patterns spell out the name Botany, but two Bold *Look* ties are prominently featured in the foreground of this ad.

In 1943, the Bold Look was already taking hold and clothing styles began to change. Lapels became wider and suit jackets were buttoning lower, allowing for more open space to display a tie. Bolder patterns began to appear on ties just as the first returning servicemen were coming home. An early type of bold tie was the panel tie, which enjoyed a brief fashion popularity around 1943. It consisted of a large vertical stripe running down the center of the tie in a color coordinated with the tie color or in a bold geometric pattern such as checks. With the success of the panel tie and other colorful tie patterns, manufacturers and designers forged ahead with the few resources available to them.

By 1948, Bold Look ties were the rage and ties joined the ranks as collectibles for the first time. Loosely based tie clubs were formed for men were not only wearing ties but collecting them, too. Noticeable were groups of musicians, movie stars, radio celebrities, and later TV personalities, all of whom enjoyed the public exposure and influence they had on popular culture. Benny Goodman, Tommy Dorsey, Rudy Vallee, Danny Kaye, Alan Ladd and other entertainers professed to be tie collectors.

Beau Brummell Ties from *Esquire*, December 1947. Early Art Deco-inspired designs from "Bold" Beau Brummell.

Manhattan shirts and ties from the *Saturday Evening Post*, May 1951.

Section from *Redbook*'s gift giving guide, December 1950. Ties include a harbor design tie by Tina Lesser and a locks design by Fath. Both are made by Signet ties.

Manhattan shirts and ties from the *Saturday Evening Post*, May 1951. The tie shown is from the Wildlife series.

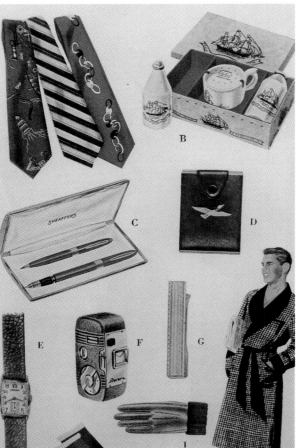

"Tell a man you like his necktie and you will see his personality unfold like a flower." - *Countess Mara from The New York Times, September 1949*

"We have learned that Mr. Charles W. Leeman, the Mayor of Omaha, is the possessor of nineteen hundred neckties, and except for a few favorites, he has not worn the same tie twice! Nor has he ever thrown a tie away. He keeps them on wooden hangers in a closet and has insured his collection for seventy five hundred dollars.

He has 100 solid reds and 600 hand-painted babies, two of which bear his portrait. For his trip to New York he brought along fourteen, and purchased a dozen while here. He has special-event ties for special events - Jack Dempsey numbers for fights; others, appropriately illustrated, for hockey, tennis, basketball, and so on. For ice shows he has a hand-painted one with a portrait of Gloria Nord, the star of Skating Vanities. Mr. Leeman showed us one of his portrait ties. It depicted him broadcasting over Station WOW. 'I wore it for the first television show in Omaha,' he said.

Mr. Leeman collects silk ties, leather ties, doeskin ties, embroidered ties, and one made of unborn calfskin. 'People used to make critical remarks about my ties being to loud,' he says, 'but public taste has caught up with me. Now I just get quiet looks of admiration.' - from the New Yorker, February 1948

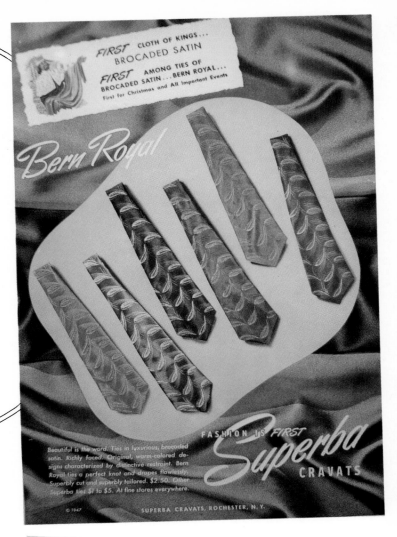

Top Right: Superba's "Bern Royal" brocaded silk ties from Esquire, December 1947.

Right: Wembley ties' assurance of quality - graphically depicted in many of their ads.

Wembley's "Winter Wonderland" designs for ties from Good Housekeeping, November 1951. Score another point for these silk and rayon beauties.

Cohama Sun Maker Ties
for Christmas from
Esquire, December 1949.

Resisto "48er" tie
from *Esquire*,
September 1948.

The Bold Look cannot be characterized by a specific design or style; it is usually highly colorful or in color combinations that were daring for the time. The earliest and most popular bold ties have designs which look back to the Art Deco style for their inspiration. Though the Art Deco geometric style is associated with the 1920s and 1930s, its decorative influence was prominently evidenced during the postwar years in many artistic fields including architectural, industrial, and commercial design. Art Deco style includes vibrant hues and exotic color combinations that influenced Bold Look tie designers. Art Deco style also had a nostalgic appeal as it inspired thoughts of life "before the war." They were good thoughts for many people.

The Bold Look included not only Art Deco geometrics but paisley patterns which underwent transformation to become bold in some unusual manifestations. Also popular were plant and floral forms from abstract tulips to swaying palm tress. Equally popular were scenes depicting hunting, fishing and western motifs with pointing setters, leaping fish, and running horses.

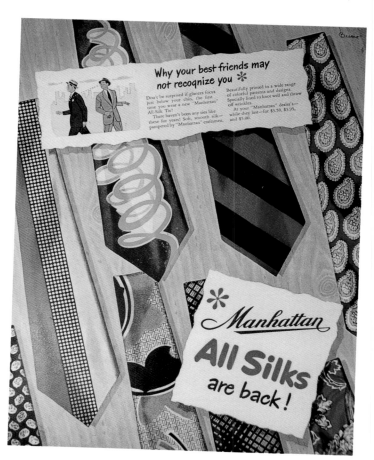

Manhattan ties from the *Saturday Evening Post*, December 1946. Both traditional and bold look are represented here

Not everyone admired Bold Look ties. Many found them garish, tasteless, and just plain loud. Critics claimed that men bemoaned the fact that women bought bold ties and forced men to wear them to keep peace in the family. Psychologists offered reasons why men should (or shouldn't) be fascinated with bold ties. The mass production of so many designs at the peak of the Bold Look's popularity might have been what we call today "overkill." An article from *Colliers* magazine in 1948 offers a different solution to the over-saturation of loud ties: "Men! No longer do you have to suffer with those loud-mouthed, ill-tempered neckties that your mother-in-law invariably gives you. A couple of brothers in Wilmington, Delaware have your salvation and are making capital out of one of the chief masculine dilemmas. Originators of a very bright post-war idea, called Tieswap, Jake and Bernard Kreshtool run a mushrooming business swapping ties. For any six of the worst neckwrappers that you send them, they'll send you six other calculated to make life more livable. The charge is one dollar."

Christmas ties from the *Saturday Evening Post*, December 1946.

for a Man's Christmas

You Can't Beat

Interwoven

Socks and Ties that Harmonize

Interwoven ties from *Good Housekeeping*, January 1952. Interwoven offered "socks and ties that harmonize."

First step in getting stuck on yourself!

GIVE YOUR EGO a lift, Man, with these lively new Arrow Ties!

We call 'em "Mirror Motifs" because they reflect smartness and A-1 styling throughout. Spend a little time before your mirror with these superb all-rayon foulards and you'll face the world with confidence, and even a dash of healthy superiority.

Arrow "Mirror Motifs" have a built-in, wrinkle-resistant lining. They tie up in a way to make Women say: "Ooooh!", and to make Men murmur: "Where'd you get it, old man, huh?"

Cluett, Peabody & Co., Inc.

$1.50

Look for the Arrow Trade-mark

Arrow ties from the *Saturday Evening Post*, May 1951. "We call them mirror motifs because they reflect smartness."

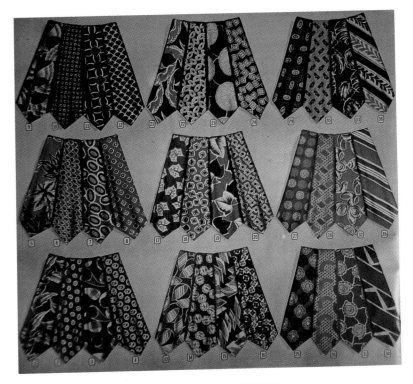

Men's fall ties from Montgomery Ward's catalog Fall-Winter 1945. This catalog probably had just gone to the presses when Victory was declared - some items and pages in the catalog are stamped "Rationed". The array of designs in the "Bold Look" reflect a war weary desire for the return of color and levity.

Boy's fall ties from Montgomery Ward's catalog Fall-Winter 1945. Besides the Bold Look tie, the catalog featured four Warner Brothers cartoon characters - Bugs, Porky, Sniffles, and Elmer.

Allover - Arrow tie with flame design; unmarked tie with heart design; unmarked tie with polka dots. These tie designs mimic traditional patterns, but the use of hearts and flames on a repetitive grid betray Bold Look sensibilities.

Allover - unmarked; marked Smoothie Ltd.; marked 65% Acetate, 35% Rayon, RN15066.

Allover - top to bottom: marked Beau Brummell "Paradise Prints", exclusive cravating; marked Beau Brummell ties the best; marked "D'elegance" Merritt Cravats, all silk. The tie on the left is unmarked.

Diagonal Stripes - all unmarked.

24

Allover pattern-
marked Grayco
End-Lock;
unmarked.

Allover - marked Cheney Cravats;
unmarked; marked Nobility, custom tailored.

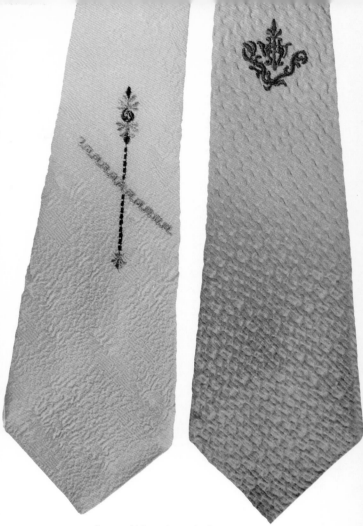

Crepe - Yellow tie marked Korry ties of California; unmarked.

Stitched Brocade - Brown marked Hollyvogue doeskin, Made in California; marked Towncraft Deluxe; marked Grayco End-Lock.

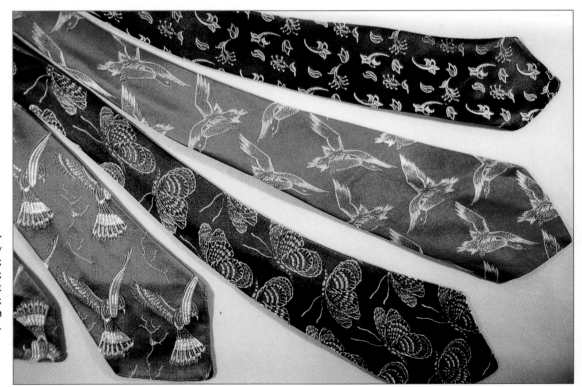

Stitched Brocade - marked Eagle design by Regal Cravats; unmarked butterfly design; duck design on Towncraft Cravats; plant forms by Fashion Craft Cravats.

Allover - all silk tie in blues; marked Artistic Cravats; pale brown floral by Hollyvogue; red, white and blue unmarked tie.

Allover - marked hand tailored, patented Feb. 27, 1923, resilient construction. 1923 is not the date of the tie but the date of the patent; marked Beau Brummell, Rayon. The design was influenced by abstract art.

Bold - all unmarked.

Paisley - unmarked; marked Regal Cravat; marked "The Persian Story" Fashion Craft Cravats; marked *Esquire* Cravat, the tie of Distinction; marked Hollyvogue doeskin, made in California.

Bold - marked Styled by Creveling of California; marked Fashion Craft Cravats; marked Fashion Craft Cravats; marked Fabric by Raxon.

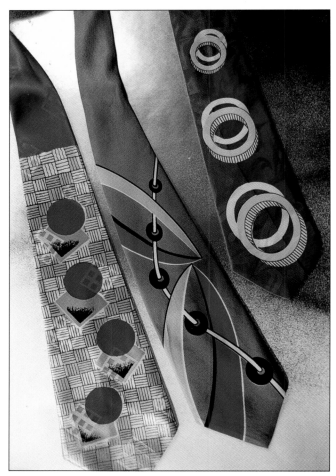

Bold - unmarked; marked Pilgrim Cravats in Zigzag design; marked Wilcrest by Wilson Brothers.

Bold - marked Fashion Craft Cravats; marked "Swing Time" by Regal Cravats; marked "Lattice Design".

Bold - marked Yellowstone prints by Wilson Brothers, fabric by Raxon; marked "Tropic" handpainted; marked made in California; unmarked.

Bold - unmarked "germ tie"; unmarked; marked Van Heusen "Van Cruse".

Bold - marked Penney's California; marked Penney's Towncraft; marked a Van Heusen Original.

Bold - unmarked brown tie; marked Pilgrim Rayon Cravats; blue and silver tie marked Haband; red, white, and blue design marked Imperial Cravats.

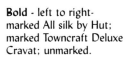

Bold - left to right-
marked All silk by Hut;
marked Towncraft Deluxe
Cravat; unmarked.

Bold - top to bottom-
unmarked; unmarked;
marked Monte Cristo
Prints in Rayon.

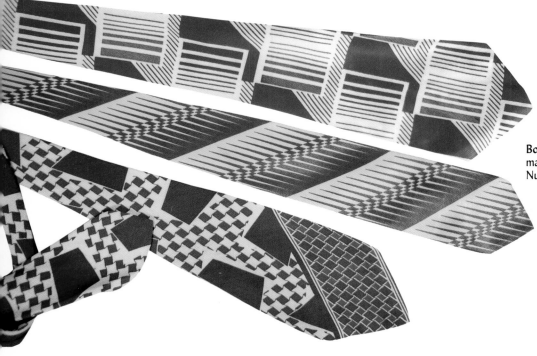

Bold - top to bottom-
marked Arrow; marked
NuWay, unmarked.

Bold - left to right- unmarked; unmarked; marked Wembley Sama Fame, a rayon fabric of Celanese yarn.

Bold - top to bottom- made of pure silk; marked made in California; marked Merritt Cravats, Longshire satins and rayons.

Bold - top to bottom- unmarked; marked Wembley; marked "Modern Age" by Haband, Patterson NJ.

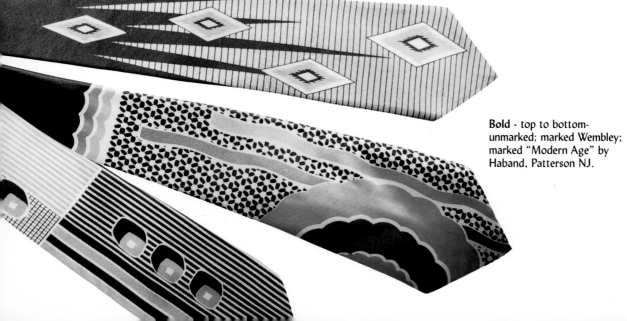

Bold - marked Creveling of California; marked Arrow;
Unmarked; marked handmade Croydon Cravat.

Bold - marked Smoothie imperial with scallop shell design;
marked Wembley; marked Yorkshire Cravats; unmarked.

Bold - All silk tie by Arrow; marked The Mary Chilton
Cravat by Spur; marked Pilgrim Cravats Deluxe, all rayon.

Bold - unmarked "amoeba" design; unmarked
"spokes" design; bird motif by Arrow.

Bold - marked Petronious Prints; marked
Esquire Cravat, the tie of distinction.

Bold - unmarked; unmarked; marked Wembley Sama
Fane, a rayon fabric of Celanese yarn; marked Arrow.

Left:
Bold - unmarked "waves and bubbles" design; unmarked; unmarked "starburst" design.

Below:
Bold - unmarked "wings" design; "Diamonds" design marked by Fashion Craft Cravats; "discs" design marked by Haband.

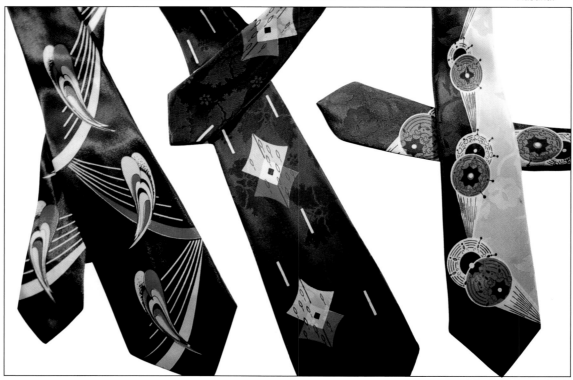

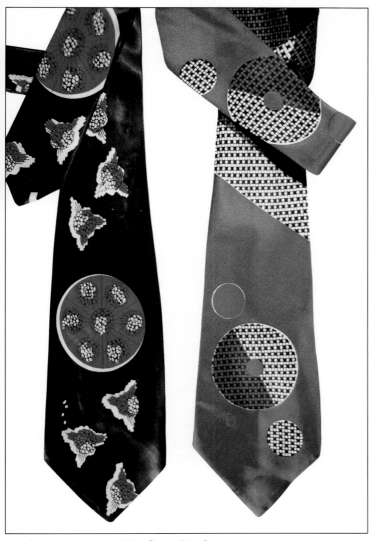

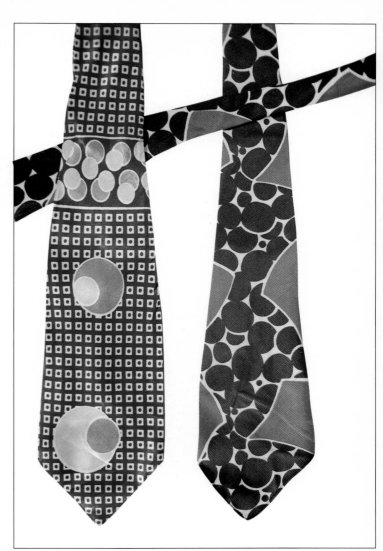

Bold - : unmarked; "Mini-Checks" by Raxon.

Bold - marked "Malibu Checks" by *Esquire* Ties of distinction; marked Wilson Brothers Duratwill fabric by Raxon.

Bold - marked Wembley; marked Wardmont; unmarked.

Bold - marked Towncraft Deluxe, resilient construction; marked Fashion Craft Cravats; marked Made and styled in California for Penney's; marked "Proton Streak" by Atomoderns.

Bold - marked Penney's Towncraft, made and styled in California; unmarked; marked Fashion Craft Cravats, Robert Brothers.

Floral - unmarked leaf design; floral design by Arrow; unmarked poppy design.

Floral - unmarked design; leaf design marked by Haband, Patterson, NJ; grape design marked "Van Splendor" by Van Heusen; milkweed design marked made and styled in California for Penney's.

Floral - unmarked leaf design; floral design marked by "English" Styled Cravats; unmarked ivy design; maple leaf design marked Chaucer Satin by Cardholm.

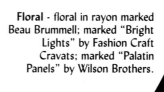

Floral - floral in rayon marked
Beau Brummell; marked "Bright
Lights" by Fashion Craft
Cravats; marked "Palatin
Panels" by Wilson Brothers.

Floral - leaf and flower design marked by
Hollyvogue, made in California; plant
design marked by Towncraft Cravats;
wheat design marked "Cal-Classics" by
Hollyvogue, made in California.

Floral - leaf design by Arrow; leaf design by Arrow:
unmarked clover design; floral design by Regal Cravats.

Floral - unmarked bamboo design; marked Wilson Brothers faultless rayon; marked Fashion Craft Cravats.

Floral - unmarked leaf design; unmarked floral and shape design; marked Penny's Towncraft, acetate.

Floral - marked "Mardi Gras" prints by Arco; marked V. Galet, Beverly Hills, all silk; marked Beau Brummell, rayon.

Floral - unmarked pleated tie; unmarked all silk floral design; floral design marked by Towncraft Deluxe.

Floral - unmarked tree design; "Timber" white birch marked by Haband, Patterson, NJ.

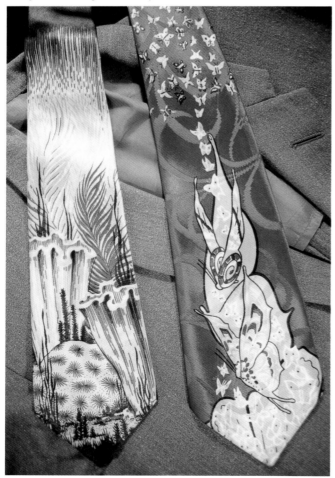

marked "Aquatones" by Merle; butterfly design marked by Wembley.

Seaweed design marked by Beau Brummell; mermaid motif by Wembley.

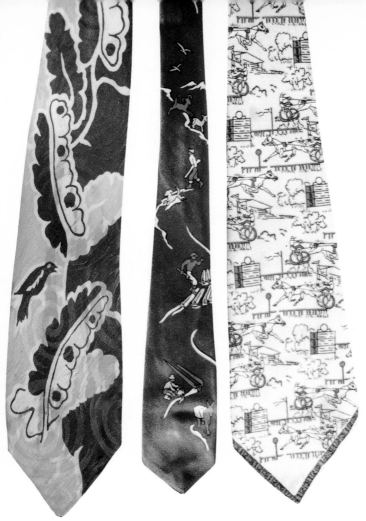

Marked Pebble Beach, made in California; marked Penney's Towncraft, mountain scene; unmarked race track motif.

Zebra design marked King Size Cravats by Spur; unicorn design marked by Creveling of California.

Apple design by Haband, Patterson, NJ; musical motif by Arco Royal.

42

Paris motif on rayon
marked Hyde Park Ties
by Manford; Paris motifs
marked Cosmopolitan.

Woodpecker design by
Vanguard Royal Cravats;
marked "Sparrow Hawk"
by Hollyvogue.

Marked "Winter Wonderland" by Wembley; marked "Snowflakes" by
Timberline Cravats; Oriental design by Arrow; hunting motif by Haband.

Maple leaf and
hummingbird design by
Pilgrim Rayon Cravats;
ducks by Fashion Craft
Cravats; unmarked tie
picturing geese in flight.

Unmarked
heraldry design;
heraldry design by
Wembley.

Unmarked paint stroke design; unmarked fleur-de-lis design; flying tire design, an awards tie that was formerly
given out annually at the Indianapolis 500 auto race awards dinners from the 1930s to the 1950s.

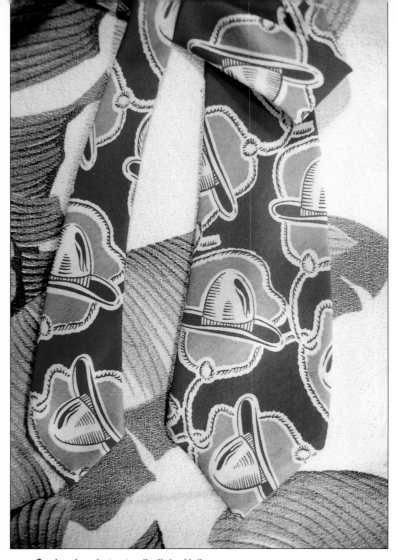

Cowboy hat design in all silk by Hollyvogue.

Film clips design on all silk tie by McCurrach.

Dice design by Stork Club; unmarked peacock design on neon pink; unmarked floral design; marked a Mary Chilton Cravat by Spur with numeral design.

Designers - Three Don Loper ties from the 1960s and 1970s.

Artistic Ties

Along with bold tie designs, artists and designers got into the act creating "artistic" ties, so that's what we will call them. Some of these ties are absolutely stunning and fetch the highest prices today. Below is a list of different categories these ties fall into, as defined by the designer, subject or medium employed:

Designer Ties

Bold Look designer ties were very different from modern "designer ties." There were only a handful of independent designers whose signatures assured quality and "artistic" design. The more prominent designers from that era whose ties you will likely encounter are:

Don Loper - He started his professional career as a dancer in the 1930s. His fashion career started when he designed the outfits for his dancing partner during their engagement at the Copacabana in New York. He moved on to Hollywood and worked as an actor and designer at the MGM studio. In 1946,

he opened a couture salon on the Sunset Strip in Hollywood. The salon moved to Beverly Hills in 1951 where it still functions as a design center. Don Loper died in 1972, but items continued to be manufactured and labeled under his name. Loper believed in "sanity in fashion" and felt clothes should never overshadow a man's personality. His ties reflect this idea and maintain a middle-of-the-road and tasteful appearance. Some may remember Don Loper's appearance in an episode of "I Love Lucy - In Hollywood" as a sunburned Lucy had to model a Don Loper dress in rough tweed at a fashion show before he would give it to her!

Countess Mara - Possibly the most recognized name in vintage designer ties is Countess Mara. She was born Lucilla de Vescovi in Rome in 1893 with no indication of a tie career in her future. In 1926 she married a wealthy textile manufacturer, Malcolm Whitman, and moved to New York with her three daughters from a previous marriage. During a breakfast

Designers - Two Don Loper ties from the 1950s.

Designers - Two ties featuring Countess Mara designs of Highland pipers and Gemini.

Designers - Two ties featuring Countess Mara designs: bamboo and crickets on green; stylized plant forms in green and white.

dispute over her husband's boring tie in 1930, the story goes, he bet she couldn't make one more interesting. Well, she did and Mr. Whitman was impressed. A star was born, but Mara's career did not begin immediately. In 1932 Mr. Whitman committed suicide and Mara was left a comfortable but emotionally torn widow. To recover her direction, she roamed Europe and decided she needed "a new baby" and ties would be it. She purchased some fabric, returned to New York, and created the first Countess Mara ties. Though successful, she felt her ties needed to be more personalized and thus she created a distinctive mark and placed it on the front of the ties. So began her career as a designer of artistic ties. Her designs became so popular that in 1938 she opened her first shop and hired art assistants. Of course she was not a real countess, but she chose the name to give her ties "snob appeal." She printed ties in limited editions which grew in numbers. Her collectible ties from the Bold Look era are decorated with a kaleidoscope of common and unusual subjects including tennis, polo, skiing, giraffes, camels, bison, lobsters, ferns, fish, deer, mermaids, shells, vultures, devils, ticker tape, cacti, fairies, fauns, flowers, dancing girls, geese, Roman heads, Egyptian heiroglyphs, astrological signs, dragonflies, mice, owls, musical instruments, sheep, zebras, safety

pins, turkeys, foxes, squirrels, clocks, guns, sea urchins, decks of cards, torn love letters, insects, key rings, circus seals, fish, and other designs. Her characteristic logo of "CM" with a crown can be found at the bottom of each tie. Though Mara's designs are often strange, her ties are never loud, due to her subtle but pleasing color palette. The Countess revealed some of her inspiration as well as her aspirations in an excerpt from a *New York Times* article of February 1949:

I think of ties morning, noon, and night. At night, if I have insomnia, I count ties instead of sheep. I seldom go to the country. For me, the country consists of the jungles of my ties. They are populated with trees, flowers, and animals. I try to make my ties colorful, interesting, artistic, and gay, rather than showy and spectacular. Shadows I see on the street sometimes give me an idea for a new design. Other manufacturers have imitated my patterns and color combinations, but I don't mind. They have expanded the acceptability of the pictorial tie, so I'm glad.

The company of Countess Mara is still operating. Since the 1980s their ties have been known more for their upscale "designer tie" image, simpler patterns, and conservative look than for her originality. Our loss.

Designers - Marked "Winged Stallion" by His Majesty, New York; Countess Mara design featuring cats and kittens.

Designers - Two ties featuring Countess Mara designs: fairies and flowers (the back says Drop those wings!); stylized floral with insects.

Tina Leser - already a noted designer of sportswear when she entered the tie market, Tina Leser's ties were manufactured by Arthur Sigman Inc. of New York. Leser ties followed a similar style of designs as her counterpart Countess Mara.

Salvador Dali - Everyone knows the name of this famous surrealist artist, but many do not know that he designed neckties. The original Dali tie designs had disturbing surrealistic images which Dali was forced to revise before they became top sellers in the 1940s and 1950s. The snob appeal of owning a tie designed by a *really* famous artist was apparent. According to knowledgable collectors, Dali or his assistants designed from a dozen to fifty different ties. Finding a Dali tie today is a tie collector's dream.

Besides the artists cited, ties can be found with the names of other designers such as Noni, Schiaparelli, Jacques Fath, Lilly Dache and Signe Gorman. Even Pablo Picasso designed a line of ties with his artwork on it. While ties by other artists of the 1940s also may appear, designer ties in the 1940s were not the extensive field they became in the 1990s.

Designers - Three Tina Leser designed ties. The one on the right is marked Atoms on the back.

Designers - A Salvador Dali designed tie marked The Road to Toledo, A Dali creation by Smoothie.

Occupied Japan Silk Ties

In the late 1940s and early 1950s, American Army troops "occupied" Japan, and among the many items produced in Japan during the occupation were silk neckties, perhaps one of the more beautiful exports. Most were hand painted but some were exquisitely embroidered. Subjects featured temples, landscapes, dragons, and animals. Some of the designs translate American idioms, but not necessarily very well. One silk necktie marked "Occupied Japan" has a humorous (but nicely painted) portrait of George Washington. Such silk ties remained popular in America through the 1950s.

Oriental - Three unmarked silk ties made for export in the 1950s. The dragon on the center tie is embroidered while the other two are hand painted.

Designers - Two Salvador Dali designed ties marked Swan Palace and Mandolin.

4. Novel-ties

This is a category of ties with odd images, lettering, characters, and gimmicks attached usually meant to produce a chuckle. The glow-in-the-dark ties are a good example and there were Christmas ties that were lit by a small battery, gag ties that squirted water, and ties with ethnic stereotypes and off-color bathroom humor. Contemporary ties with licensed pop culture figures on them are sometimes also called novelty ties.

Specialties - Footprints on front of tie lead to outhouse on back.

Glow-in-the-dark necktie from *Jingle Jangle Comics*, April 1946. When the war was over, the patriotic glow-in-the-dark victory tie became the fun-loving glowing-kiss-me necktie. By day, a lovely swank tie... by night, a call to love in glowing words.

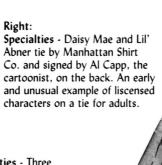

Right:
Specialties - Daisy Mae and Lil' Abner tie by Manhattan Shirt Co. and signed by Al Capp, the cartoonist, on the back. An early and unusual example of liscensed characters on a tie for adults.

Left:
Specialties - Three mirror-image ties. When the fat end of the tie is held facing left, the design reveals lettering: Northwest Builds Best, Thor Nashland, and Bullshit. These could be Retro.

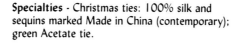

Specialties - Christmas ties: 100% silk and sequins marked Made in China (contemporary); green Acetate tie.

Regal Ties from *Esquire*, December 1947. To sell men's ties, sex appeal had the same effect as "girlie" designs.

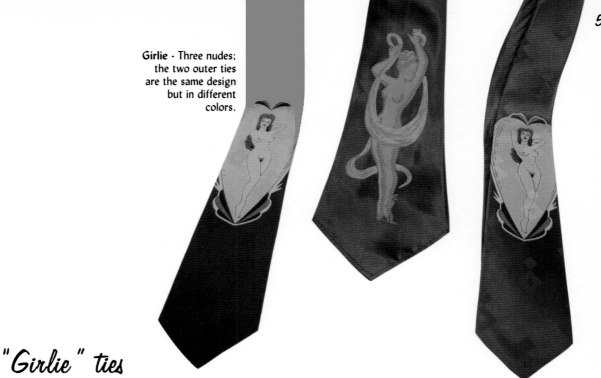

Girlie - Three nudes; the two outer ties are the same design but in different colors.

"Girlie" ties

Probably the most phallic item of a man's clothing is his necktie, so what better place to put a pretty girl than on a necktie! The 1940s and 1950s were the heyday of pretty "pin-up art" which flourished on prints and calenders by such artists as Vargas, Petty, Armstrong, and Elvgren, all of whom acquired dedicated followers. There were also lesser artists who painted alluring women on ties, and some were quite lascivious. The more risque nudes were placed on ties so that only the head and shoulders would appear when the man's jacket was buttoned. These "girlies" also appeared on the backs of ties and they are called "peek-a-boos," many featuring screened photos of semi-naked and naked women. These photos are on the inside lining of the wide end of the tie, and the outside of the tie is usually a solid color with simple decorations. The "peek-a-boo" ties fetch a high price today; any tie with "girlies" or "nudies" are much sought after.

Girlie - Acetate tie featuring screen-printed woman with a scotty dog; nubile beauty painted by hand on rayon tie; printed rayon bathing beauty tie.

CELEBRI-TIES
with SPECS APPEAL

Have fun wherever you wear her. *The tie with three-dimensions!* A startling effect created by real gold-rimmed sunglasses worn by hand painted Hollywood lovelies—on a background of beautiful crepe. The "something different" gift. Ties in blue, wine, brown, tan and gray. Choice of platinum blonde, blonde and red-head. **$1 50**

Ask for it at your favorite store—or send check or money order to: **Harry Geiss Products Inc., 230 5th Ave., N. Y. 1, N. Y.** Specify model and color.

The Celebri-Tie with Specs Appeal! from *Esquire*, July 1949.

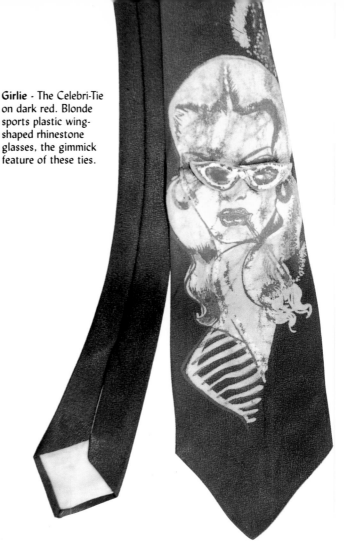

Girlie - The Celebri-Tie on dark red. Blonde sports plastic wing-shaped rhinestone glasses, the gimmick feature of these ties.

Left:
Girlie - The Celebri-Tie on brown. Redhead sports green plastic glasses. On original package is marked Resisto Tie Co.

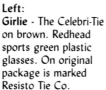

Right:
Girlie - Peek-A-Boo ties. Popular in the 1950s, these innocent outside designs revealed a titillating secret on the inside back. Many featured outright photographic nudes. This tame example is marked "Ballerinas" by Nuway.

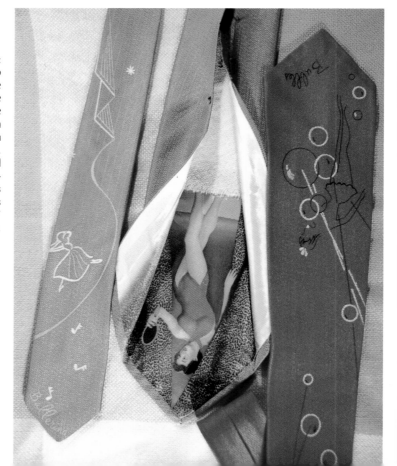

Hand-painted ties

Hand-painted ties include many different mediums used to paint or print a design on a tie. They are mentioned separately here because understanding them increases one's appreciation.

Painted by hand - the artist uses the tie as a canvas and paints directly on it. This method was popular during the 1940s when ties were scarce. The method appealed to home hobbyists with a creative bent. But note: Not all ties that say "hand-painted" are painted by hand. Many ties that are marked "hand-painted" were actually screen printed (see below).

Screen printing - the design is printed on the tie by a silk screen process. Most of the screen printed ties had images first drawn by artists, then screen printed onto the tie, and finally hand-tinted (colored) by a different artist or worker, making them officially "hand-painted."

Handpainted - Two designs with "streaks". Marked handpainted in California, acetate woven with nylon; marked on back California Artists Guild and signed on front.

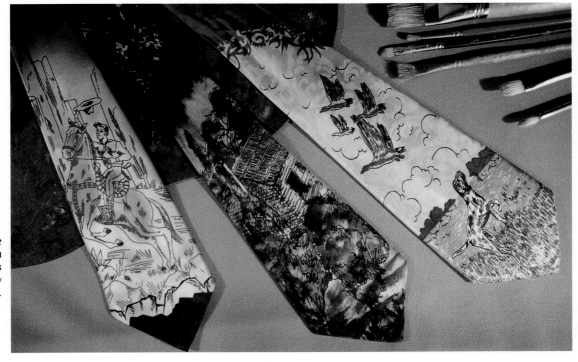

Handpainted - Three screen-printed ties with tinting. The middle tie is marked Masterpieces by Regal Cravats.

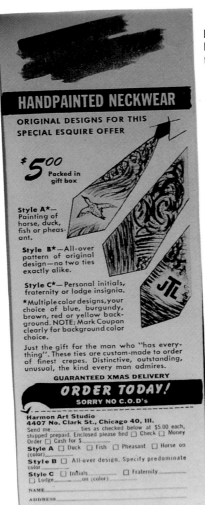

Handpainted - Ties by Harmon Art Studio, Chicago from *Esquire*, 1947.

Handpainted - Two horse motifs with streaks. Marked Handpainted in California, acetate woven with nylon; marked Painted by Hand, Pilgrim Cravats, resilient construction.

Handpainted - three ties with streaks. Marked designed at Blue Bird Studios; marked Painted by Hand for National Shirt Shops; marked painted in California of nylon and acetate by Creveling.

Handpainted - streaks! Resort scene tie marked woven with nylon; palm tree tie marked Penney's Towncraft; Mardi Gras scene marked handpainted nylon and acetate.

Handpainted - Two handpainted beauties: pure silk flowering cactus tie handpainted by Mark of California; unmarked horse and cowboy design on rayon.

Handpainted - Three ties with streaks. Leaf design marked Handpainted in California, a Towncraft Deluxe Cravat; deer tie by Pilgrim Cravats; unmarked pheasant tie.

Handpainted - Screen printed initial "E"; painted by hand oranges design by Hollyvogue; screen printed Venice scenes marked "Painted Classics" by Arco.

Handpainted - Three painted by hand. Amoeba shape design by Wembley; marked Fashion Craft Cravats; unmarked feather design.

Handpainted - Two painted-by-hand ties: cowboy by Hollyvogue, a California original; bulldog design hand tailored by Andre of California.

Right:
Handpainted - Duck hunting scene marked "Hunters Delight", the classics by Park Lane; signed on back "created by Imogene, San Francisco, Calif". All silk.

Above:
Handpainted - Two ties with fishing motifs: unmarked fish and landscape design; marked "Rainbow Trout" by Signe Gorman, artist, a Colorcade Print by Cutter Cravats.

Handpainted - Painted by hand horse by Penney's Towncraft; marked Hand painted in California, Acetate woven with Nylon; painted by hand fishing lures on unmarked tie.

Airbrush - in recent decades, may people have become familiar with airbrush "art" on rock album covers, customized cars, or t-shirt designs. It has only been 25 years since the use of the airbrush became an artistic medium. Before this, the airbrush was used primarily as a tool to retouch and color photographs and for technical illustration. In the Bold Look era, this tool was used with ties somewhat frugally. Examples shown here are typical of the air-brushed designs of the 1940s.

To visualize how an airbrush works, think of a miniaturized and highly refined spray paint can. The airbrush is used, with greater control, like a large, hand-held pen attached to an air compressor.

Glitter and Coralene- two mediums used occasionally on ties which today are gaining popularity with tie collectors. Glitter was applied sparingly over hand-painted designs to enhance the effect. Today, you will not find much glitter on ties as most of the glue used has dried, causing the glitter to fall off. Coralene is a more fascinating paint medium than glitter. Fine glass beads (the consistency of sand) are applied with glue over an already-painted design. The technique creates a beautifully subtle iridescence. Although hard to appreciate in a photograph, coralene can be compared with the effect of a bicycle or highway reflector.

Handpainted - three ties using airbrush and other techniques: floral design marked Towncraft Deluxe; unmarked design; unmarked leaves design.

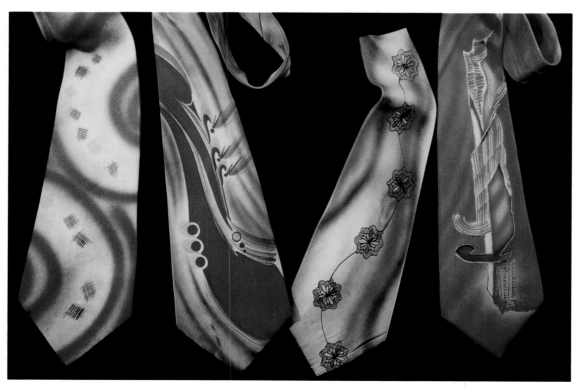

Handpainted - Four ties using airbrush with other techniques. Wembley; abstract marked handpainted in California; unmarked floral design; unmarked abstract design.

Handpainted - Four unmarked ties using airbrush with other techniques.

Handpainted - Unmarked glitter and screen-printed palm tree design; unmarked glitter and screen-printed spider web design; "coralene" parrot design marked Adriaan of California; unmarked screen-printed fish design.

Handpainted - All designs feature "coralene" style: marked Timberline Cravats; abstract design marked made and styled in California for Penney's; fishing lures design by Regal Cravats; game bird design marked 55% acetate / 45% rayon RN 16546.

5. Fif-ties Skinnies

Renuzit Spot Remover from
Good Housekeeping, June 1950.

In the early 1950s, men's ties took a decidedly conservative turn. As post-war optimism faded, strikes, recessions, the Korean War and the fear of communism caused many people, especially in America, to adopt restrained, conformist lives. The spunk of the post-war world and its encouragement to be an individual was replaced by a desire to blend in and not upset the status quo. Tie designs quietly and slowly faded, until by the mid-1950s a Bold Look tie seemed already dated; the narrow tie replaced it.

The new narrow tie now followed the edicts of a restrained, trimmer style. By the mid-1950s, narrow ties became skinny ties that did not exceed three-inch widths. Skinny ties were extremely popular with teenagers, college kids, and the people they idolized. Elvis Pressley, James Dean and most of the other rock n' roll stars of the period wore skinny ties. The narrow tie would change in design over the years, but it retained its popularity well into the 1960s.

"Fifties" ties, whether skinny or regular in width, could be found in a myriad of styles. Solid colors and stripes returned along with other various traditional patterns. Woven and crocheted ties again became popular and wool was once more "in". The "nubby touch" ties of coarse silk and fabrics with soft, irregular textures enjoyed attention. Dacron polyester made ties easier to wash and new chemical fabric protectors (such as Scotchgard) made stains easy to remove. Narrow ties sporting horizontal striping in staid colors with squared bottoms were a hit.

But by the mid-1950s, the most conservative part of the decade was over and a new, more colorful era had begun. Foreign neckwear was again commonplace in America and the ties from Europe put American designers to shame. Paris ties offered pictorial designs, famous paintings, graduated stripes, and swirl designs. Italian ties offered wonderful black and gold combinations and English ties (which had the first patented blended fabric) now offered blends of incredible materials. The European influence on American fashions returned in full force by the early 1960s.

Wembley Ties from
Good Housekeeping,
June 1957.

Cavalier Ties from *Good Housekeeping*, July 1957.

Palm Beach Ties
by Beau Brummell
from *Good
Housekeeping*,
June 1954.

Palm Beach Ties
by Beau Brummell
from *Good
Housekeeping*,
May 1954.

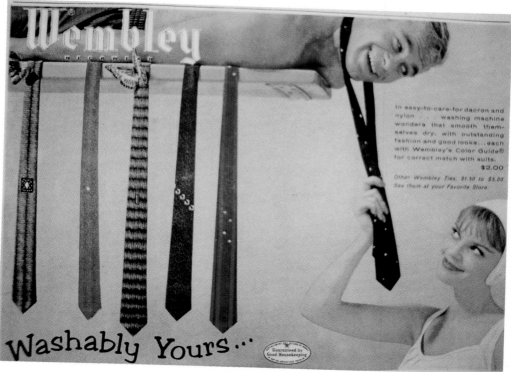

Wembley Ties from *Good Housekeeping*, June 1959.

Pre-Skinny - Two scotty dog designs by Coplan, 100% Acetate, RN 19117; horse design tie by Park Avenue Aristocrat.

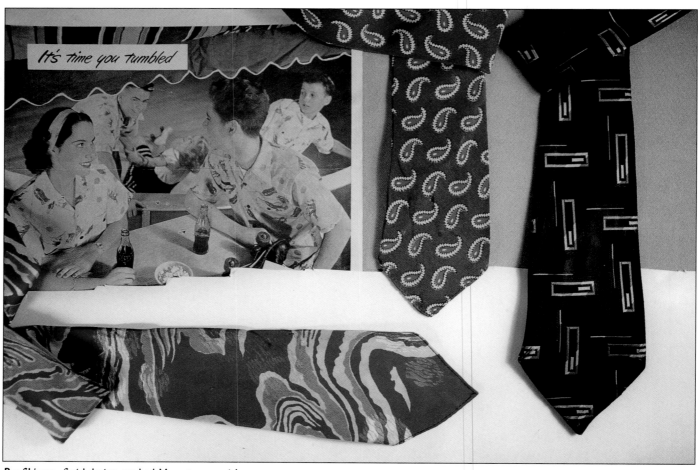

Pre-Skinny - Swirl design marked Murrytown; paisleys marked Pilgrim Cravats; unmarked tie with rectangles.

Pre-Skinny - Three medium width rayon acetate ties: right marked Arrow. two unmarked.

Pre-Skinny - Allover design marked Croydon Cravats, all silk; striped and swirls ties are both unmarked.

Pre-Skinny - Three ties with polka dot designs: left unmarked; two marked Park Avenue Aristocrat Cravat.

64

Pre-Skinny -
Marked Wembley;
marked Cervantes
all silk; marked all
silk; unmarked.

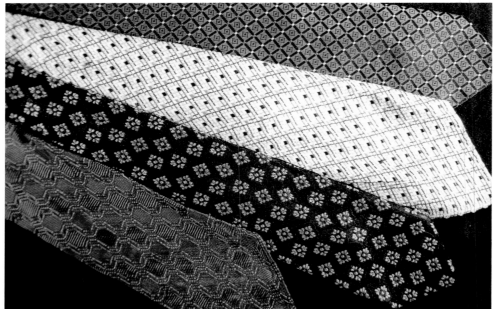

Pre-Skinny - Green and brown
unmarked tie; marked Haband
all Acetate; marked hand
made by Relasto; marked
Haband Dacron Polyester.

Pre-Skinny - Three silk
ties with the same
pattern in green, brown,
and yellow marked Park
Avenue WPL9302.

Pre-Skinny - Star design tie marked DiTucci Silk; unmarked modern design; unmarked handpainted abstract design; marked Penney's Towncraft, made in California.

Pre-Skinny - Acetate tie with allover arrow design marked Wilson Brothers; all silk tie marked by Dupre Resilio; marked all silk; marked Pilgrim Acetate Cravats.

66

Pre-Skinny - Boy's "ready-tied" ties marked Sta-Ti, US patent 2066126.

Pre-Skinny - Car motif tie marked by Park Lane; unmarked; marked Croydon Cravats.

Pre-Skinny - Four ties with various diagonal stripes. The bottom left tie in red and black has a paper label which reads, "It's shape holding because there's PELLON inside, wrinkle resistant miracle interlining"; The bottom right tie is marked Made in Hollywood.

Pre-Skinny - Two clip-on ties. Both are made of silk.

Pre-Skinny - Woven ties, left marked Resilio; blue tie with arrows marked hand woven Indian Cravats, Sandia Weavers.

Pre-Skinny - Two clip-on ties. Both are made of silk.

68

"The necktie has a destiny of art and love. We must defend it, for it is the only silent language we've preserved for addressing women . . . for enticing them with symbols of art, which are the most fitting. All honor to the universal father, Adam, the first man to wear a tie, making it from the green of the grape leaf and the red of the offending apple." - from Americas Magazine, August 1951

Traditional - Diagonal stripe unmarked; marked Beau Brummell 50% Dacron / 50% wool, WPL 124; unmarked; bottom tie marked Superba 50% polyester / 50% wool, WPL 2831.

Traditional - Assortment of standard diagonal striped ties.

"However, the necktie floats like the shipwrecked sailor's bottle with a message in it. It survives as a symbol of the need of the libido, linked so fundamentally to biology. The necktie is a flag, an anarchistic flag, in the middle of the chest, where everyone says what he pleases, protesting against the monotonous suit he wears. It is more than a call from man to woman or a guarantee of the perpetuation of the species. It is also a symbol of the personality and even the esthetic category of the man who drapes it around his neck. With it we shun the chorus and recite our monologue."
- from Americas Magazine, August 1951

Traditional - Three silk ties with various designs.

Traditional - Marked Clipper, made in Chile; Clipper, made in Chile; Cutter Cravat 65% rayon / 35% silk.

"New, narrower-width ties, from 2.5 to 3 inches, balance the new men's shirt styles. And tie patterns which have the design placed high under the tie knot call attention to trim collars. You'll find simple or elaborate embroidered, painted and woven designs as well as bands of contrasting color and fabric. There's a version for every taste." - from McCalls Magazine, October 1953

Right:
Skinny - Unmarked; marked 65% acetate / 35% rayon, RN 18970; blue tie with striping, marked Trimshape by Cavalier of Louisville, patent # 2499206.

Below:
Skinny - An assortment of ties with horizontal stripes, all marked Ernst of San Francisco.

"Neckties. They're what I collect. A rather odd item to collect, I admit, but no more unusual than, say, shaving mugs, snuff boxes, old handbills, or candlesticks. As of today, my neckties number more than 1,200 and each holds a special interest for me. The ties in my collection are not only for display - they are also to be worn. And with so many to choose from, it is hard sometimes to make a selection. What do I do when I can't make up my mind? Why, I just go out and buy another tie." - Mr. John E. Howard of Grand Forks, North Dakota. from the "Hobby Hitching Post" in the Rotarian Magazine, November 1952

Skinny - Five examples of Smoothie's "Button Down Tie" clip-ons. The back flaps of the ties have buttonholes in them to attach to a shirt button.

Skinny - An assortment of ties with horizontal stripes, a style popular in skinny ties.

Skinny - Marked
Hinomaru, Tokyo;
unmarked; all wool
RN 33585.

Skinny - Horse motifs.
Silver tie marked
Rhodes; all silk blue tie
marked Arrow;
unmarked tie with
knight design.

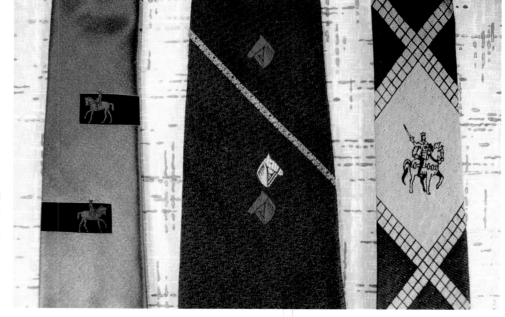

Skinny - an assortment
of ties in red, black and
white. : marked Arrow;
marked Casa Rio, all silk,
RN 16226; unmarked;
marked Casa Rio, all silk,
RN 16226; marked all
silk WPL 3116.

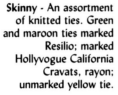

Skinny - An assortment of knitted ties. Green and maroon ties marked Resilio; marked Hollyvogue California Cravats, rayon; unmarked yellow tie.

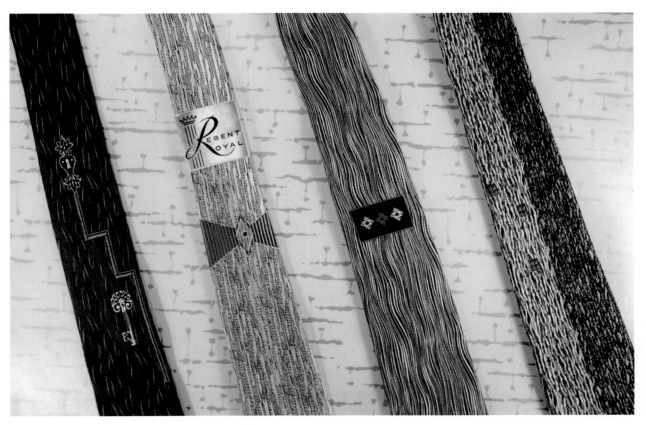

Skinny - Four ties with striated vertical patterns. Marked Made in California 100% rayon, RN 16596; original paper label reads Royal Regent; marked Arrow Kwik-Klip; marked All silk by Damon.

Left:
Skinny - The Graphic Look. All marked Fashion Craft Cravats except second from left tie marked Arrow.

Next Page:
Skinny - Vehicle motifs. Race car design on pale blue-green tie marked Wembley imported Priestleys Nor East; horse and carriage design on red tie marked Silk tissue grenadine; old buggy design on unmarked tie; Penney's Towncraft tie depicts horseless carriages, sleek Cadillacs and skyscrapers.

Skinny - Three ties in blues with red and white designs. The tie on the left is marked Haband's Dacron.

Skinny - Horizontal designs. Dark blue tie marked Woven in Italy; cowboy motifs on tie marked Macy's California; all silk tie in browns with little demons; unmarked tie with palm tree motif.

Skinny - the Graphic Look. Unmarked yellow tie; marked Penney's Towncraft, made and styled in California; unmarked tan tie with flourishes; marked Pilgrim Cravats, Sears, Roebuck and Co.

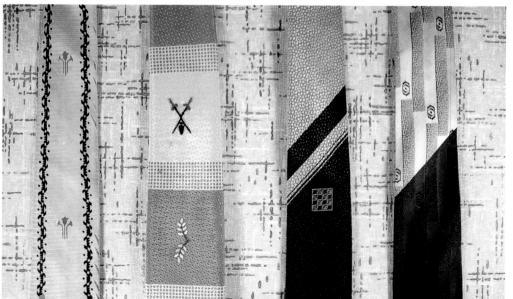

Skinny - Unmarked; unmarked tie with crossed swords design; unmarked; marked Fifth Avenue Cravats Deluxe.

Skinny - The Graphic Look. All ties are unmarked except the green tie with white flourishes which is marked Jarnac Resilio, all silk.

Skinny - The Graphic Look. All ties are unmarked except the black tie with white fleur-de-lis which is marked Custom Craft Cravats.

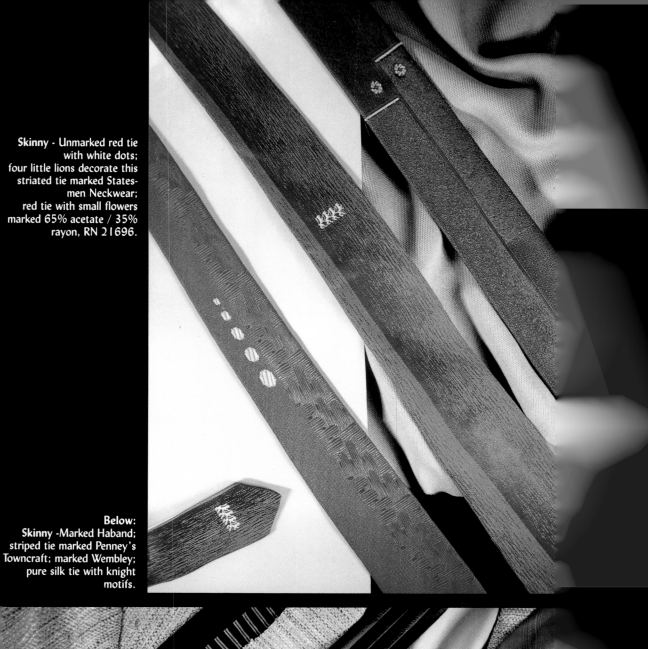

Skinny - Unmarked red tie with white dots; four little lions decorate this striated tie marked Statesmen Neckwear; red tie with small flowers marked 65% acetate / 35% rayon, RN 21696.

Below:
Skinny -Marked Haband; striped tie marked Penney's Towncraft; marked Wembley; pure silk tie with knight motifs.

"If you have the man, Stern's has his regimental and divisional pure silk ties. Inspired by the insignia and the colors of regiments and division of the US and British Armed Forces of both world wars. Yes, actually if you have a man who saw service in either war, Stern's has his special unit tie. 96 separate color combinations representing 287 different military units. Each tie label carries his correct unit number. What better Valentine?"
- Ad for Stern Brothers clothes from the New Yorker, February 1950

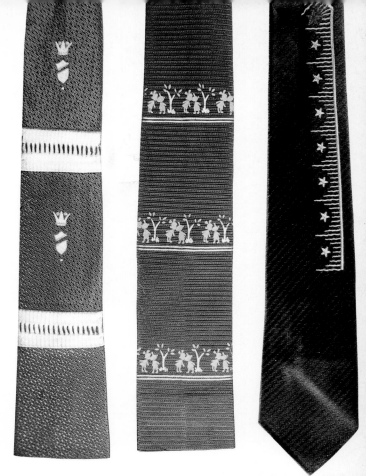

Skinny - Unmarked; horizontal design of children kissing by Pilgrim Cravats, all Acetate; unmarked brown tie with star design.

Below:
Skinny - all ties are unmarked except the dark tie on the right which is marked 65% rayon / 35% silk, RN 19225.

Skinny - Unmarked gold tie; marked Apre, all silk; marked Wembley Golden House, all silk; dark tie marked all silk, RN 19881.

Skinny - Marked Wembley; 100% acetate tie in striated design; marked a Haband tie, Patterson NJ, Sheen Gabardine by Mallinson of Fifth Avenue.

Skinny - The Graphic Look. The dark brown tie on the left is marked A Riviera Creation by Pilgrim; the third tie with vertical striping is marked Rhynecliffe, hand-made with the dots.

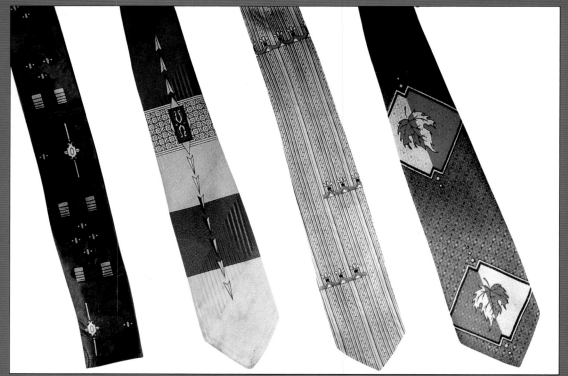

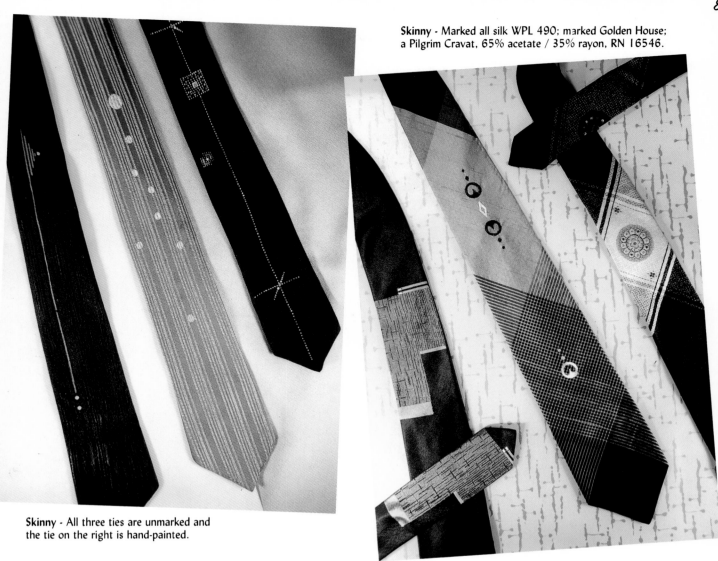

Skinny - Marked all silk WPL 490; marked Golden House; a Pilgrim Cravat, 65% acetate / 35% rayon, RN 16546.

Skinny - All three ties are unmarked and the tie on the right is hand-painted.

Skinny - Marked A Van Heusen Original; Wembley tie with spider web design; unmarked black tie with pink and white designs; unmarked pink tie.

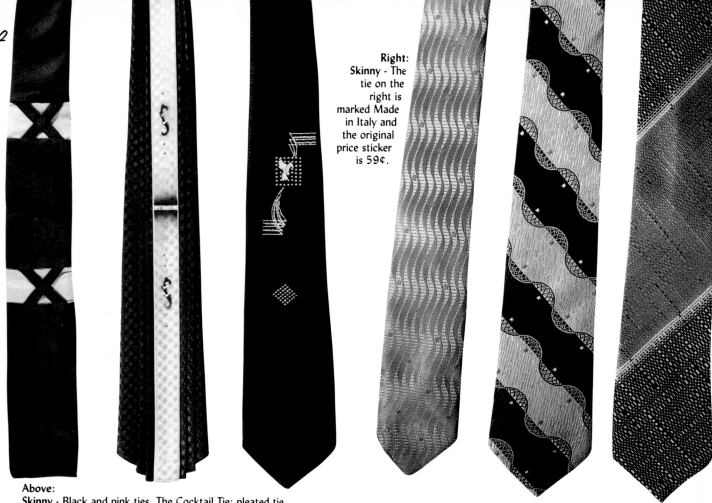

Right:
Skinny - The tie on the right is marked Made in Italy and the original price sticker is 59¢.

Above:
Skinny - Black and pink ties. The Cocktail Tie; pleated tie marked Penney's Towncraft (10); unmarked tie with bird design.

Skinny - Unmarked dark blue tie; silver/blue tie marked Dunhill by Straford; unmarked blue tie with white stripes; marked Fashion Craft WPL 2555; dark tie marked 65% acetate / 35% rayon, RN 21254; Croydon rayon and silk, WPL 1007.

6. Six-ties Kippers

During the early 1960s, men's neckwear might be described as "stale." Ties from this period do not offer new styling or original designs that differ from ties of the 1950s. Stripes, plaids and solids held sway and skinny ties got even narrower, reaching a mere 2 inches in width. A Superba tie advertisement from 1965 shows two narrow ties, one in red and black stripes and the other in brown with the standard minimal design in the center; they harken to the fifties styles. If we follow the "calm-before-the-storm" theory, we could expect the next wave of ties to be bold once more.

British designers played an influential role in American fashions of the 1960s. In the beginning of the decade, the British style dictated what it had through the 1950s - narrow lapel suits, button down shirts, and moderately proportioned ties in neat figures or regimental stripes. Also

Superba Cravats from *Esquire*, September 1965. These drab examples met stiff competition a few years later when the Peacock Look arrived.

popular were British tweeds and hefty wool plus Scottish plaids. But tie styles finally started to change. In 1964, silk ascots became the rage and presented a dire challenge to neckties. The huge popularity of turtle neck shirts and sweaters, first popularized by the bohemian "beatniks" of the 1950s and early 1960s, had the tie industry, already in a slump, wondering if it would survive the fashion changes. But no fear, for the British were about to export a tie that would instigate the next wave of exuberance in neckwear; the mid-1960s was the period of "swinging England." Everything of fashion coming from London, in particular, was quickly translated into a new statement. Then, as always, the youth culture was instilled in popular fashion. The Beatles, Twiggy, Mods and Rockers, and Carnaby Street all were quickly exported to America where teenagers and young twenty-somethings quickly embraced an eye popping, new image. The "mod" (for "modern") look was the Americanized version of British "mods'"

Rooster's Heatherknit line. Rooster was one of the first companies to offer square end ties in the 1950s.

taste for Regency coats, ascots, and high boots. But most importantly to the neckwear world, the kipper tie appeared. Created in England around 1965, the kipper was wide, as wide as the Bold Look ties had been in the forties. Kippers sported patterns previously considered unsuitable or too effeminate for men such as small pastel florals, chintzes, and abstract designs in vivid colors. The kipper tie found acceptance in a broad range of English men who found its designs appealing.

The fashion industry and its publications in America were quick to embrace the imported kippers. America was going through cultural and fashion changes such that op (short for "optical") art began to appear on wallpaper, bedspreads, and drinking glasses alike. The eye-twisting effect of black and white optical designs showed up in fashion and even was made it onto ties. The rise of pop (as in "popular") art, on the other hand, was even more influential and created a whole new way of seeing ordinary objects as icons. Pop art paintings were bold, graphic and colorful. Andy Warhol's soup cans started appearing on jackets, bedsheets, posters, and even (yes) ties. It was the "graphic" aspect that gave this period's look its uniqueness. In New York, Push Pin Studios started creating advertising images as well as art posters with heavily outlined, stylized images in vibrant colors and this style became exemplified best by artist Peter Max. Max's posters and books started appearing with the dawn of the "hippie" (as being "hip" or "in style") movement and he was very popular with that crowd. Someone saw commercial potential in his work and by the late 1960s Peter Max designs were embellished on every conceivable object. Yes, he did decorate clothing and a line of ties, too. Max followed the pop art credo and put his colorful, wild designs on everyday objects such as wastebaskets, pillowcases, watchbands and sneakers, to name a few.

In the midst of op, pop, and mod came the hippie movement. The hippie's rejection of the traditional American values and lifestyle created a non-style. Along with everything else,

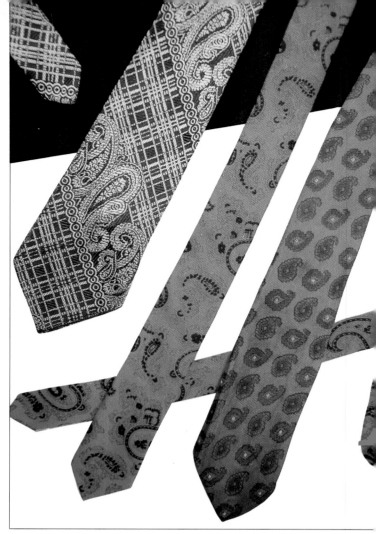

Three ties with paisleys. All silk blue and silver tie marked Rhodia, RN 19970; day-glo pink cotton tie marked Designed in Italy by Angelo Correlli, RN 15500; marked Brooks Brothers, all silk printed in England.

Various ties with diagonal stripes. Unmarked metallic brocade; gold and red striped tie marked 65% wool / 35% silk, RN 17597. Original price tag reads $2.50; marked Bardini, all silk imported fabric.

hippies rejected the established fashions people were persuaded to wear by calling them "uniforms." Ties were seen by them as too conventional and were quickly dumped on the reject pile. (Two exceptions should be mentioned: many men in hippie or rock bands wore a Bold Look tie on stage for a "campy" effect, and many hippie women with sewing skills ravaged thrift stores for old Bold Look ties (10¢ apiece back then) and created quilts, skirts, and shirts from them. Cut up, ties also made colorful patches on denim blue jeans (the real "uniforms" of conformity). Hippies replaced ties with beads, necklaces and scarfs. Hippie culture also favored "psychedelic" art with its drug-induced, hallucinogenic, pulsating, and fluorescent colors. The original hippies would never have

Unmarked grid design; "mod" wool tie marked designed by John Stephens, Carnaby Street, London, hand-crocheted in Malta; cotton tie with compasses marked Rooster, WPL 13303; silk tie marked Christian Dior; winged horse design on unmarked tie.

imagined that their rejection of society and everything they favored actually would become the major fashion trend of another day, worldwide! Though not always embracing the hippie lifestyle, many men adopted the counter-culture, non-traditional appearance that went with it. More importantly, what transferred from the hippie ethos to the world at large was the anti-taste, anti-fashion, and "do your own thing" attitude.

Meanwhile, back in the Establishment and traditional fashion world, the necktie was undergoing a struggle to re-invent itself. Shirt designer Barry Booneshaft was among the first American designers to introduce solid colored dress shirts in purple, green, and yellow hues, etc. Once color went wild on shirts, ties could be bolder to harmonize. Pierre Cardin, a young Parisian designer, is credited with exporting the first of the new floral ties to America. Ralph Lauren, who started his fashion designing career as a tie designer, helped to popularize wider ties in the late 1960s. Growing interest in nostalgia was influential, too, and the release of the movie *Bonnie and Clyde*, about famous outlaw non-conformists of the 1930s, created a new popularity for retro ties styled after neckwear of the '20s, '30s and '40s. Despite this sudden interest again in neckties, the tie industry was holding its breath. The final blow to the onslaught of ascots, dickies, turtlenecks, scarfs, neckerchiefs, and beads was the anti-establishment message of re-inventing or discarding old traditions. Many in the industry feared the "anything goes" attitude would result in the disappearance of the archetypal, but functionless, necktie. One designer even predicted there would be no ties or collars in 1980!

Handwoven Indian Madras cotton tie marked Rooster; peace tie marked Rooster by Sun Fabrics, WPL 13303; unmarked acetate tie; op art tie marked Schiaparelli.

Marked Rhodia Acetate imported fabric, RN 22227; red silk tie with stripes marked Bronzini; orange and green tie marked Mr. John.

"At present you can pick from an especially attractive array of ties. Trends are running a gamut from conservative "all-over-neat" styles and solids with small "under-the-knot" designs to bright paisley and batik designs. Paisley with a yellow background is popular with young college and business men. Wool ties with a hand woven look in muted tweeds, plaids and stripes are in great demand, as are iridescent and lustrous textures. Neckties with square ends are growing in favor as well." - from Good Housekeeping, December 1965

Below: Indian print tie marked The Bum Steer Ltd; polka dots marked Crackerjacks; unmarked tie with pop art graphics; barber pole striped cotton tie in hot pink and gold marked Made in Hong Kong.

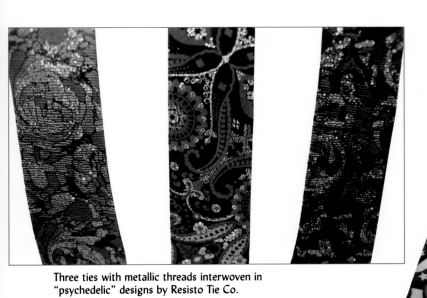

Three ties with metallic threads interwoven in "psychedelic" designs by Resisto Tie Co.

Two ties by Resisto, one featuring a USA patriotic design and the other a bold peace sign.

Three paisley ties marked Lord Aubrey, Great Britain; marked 65% Dacron Polyester 35% cotton, RN 28100; marked Made and woven in England.

7. Seven-ties Peacock

When the dust of the 1960s settled, a few things were apparent:

The fashion revolution of the 1960s had played itself out. With too many choices (fashion vs. anti-fashion and rules-were-made-to-be-broken attitudes), confusion reigned and the fashion industry spent most of the decade making desperate stabs at trying to dictate fashion and at the same time keep order.

The tie industry *did* survive the atomic attack of neck competition and continue to flourish to this day (while turtlenecks have yet to return). Shirts and jackets did not become obsolete - which was a good sign for the tie folks. What did perish was the concept of distinctly different clothes only appropriate for certain parts of the day and situations. *Esquire Magazine* surveyed the situation in 1971 and reported:

> A plaid sports jacket and checkered slacks worn with a patterned tie? Of course. It's all part of man's liberation from the drab unimaginativeness of his apparel. In shirts and ties it has reached a point where there is no longer any clear-cut distinction between what is appropriate for the boardroom and what for the discotheque.

Eagle shirts and ties from *Esquire*, September 1970. Tie is priced in ad at $10.00.

Vietnam, oil embargos, Watergate, recessions - even the Beatles breaking up in 1970 seemed to signal a new, more focused era. The 1960s had been the experimental phase. In the 1970s, bell-bottom pants, recreational drugs, and bold, "anything goes" designs became assimilated into the mainstream culture in America. The majority of the youth who had embraced the hippy look, but not the lifestyle, put their love beads in a box and went out and got jobs.

The new wide tie, from *Esquire*, 1970.

Maveat suits showing a man sporting a scarf
instead of a tie, from *Esquire*, September 1970.

Wembley ties from *Esquire*, July 1976.

The Peacock Look was coined by the fashion industry in the late 1960s. It, of course, refers to the male peacock spreading his tail feathers to attract the female. It seemed that men were dressing like peacocks, and they were. For the first time in decades, the low infant mortality rate and the baby boom of the late 1940s had created an imbalance of more adult males than females in the 1970s. So men were dressing up to be individuals in competition with one another. There also was fallout from the styles of the 1960s - men then did not reject ties and shirts, just the rules that dictated what was acceptable. Along with this came a sexual revolution in fashion which culminated in the "unisex" look. Women's fashions had borrowed from men's fashions in the past, but now this was seen as a bold, "anything goes" feminist statement. Conversely, men's fashions displayed idioms associated with female attire such as large scarves in bold prints, blousy shirts in bright colors, more jewelry and accessories (who remembers purses for men?), beaded belts, shoulder bags, and thick, high-heeled shoes.

The designs on Peacock Look ties were not all post-psychedelic butterflies. Diagonal stripes, in forms never seen before, were among the most common designs on these ties. Paisleys enjoyed fresh interpretations and all-over designs featured images besides geometric shapes. An article in *Department Store Management* of October, 1971, presented the popular styles: "The rising appeal of rich textures in clothing is nowhere more boldly manifested than in the neckwear fabrics. Knits, velvets, heavy wools, raw silks, and rugged cottons will all vie for the fashion dollar. Motifs will run rampant across many designs: nostalgic animals, romantic fretwork, Neo-Classic scenes and the great outdoors."

Shape and fabric have important roles in Peacock ties. The width of ties reached a maximum of 5.5 inches, settling on 5 inches as a standard. Peacock ties are about 3/4 of an inch wider than the Bold Look ties and the wider shape created a bigger knot. Big Peacock ties looked perfectly normal with the long tapered shirt collars and wide jacket lapels. The fabrics of Peacock ties are also distinguishable, with polyester most often associated with this look. Polyester was often blended with silk, rayon, acetate, and nylon, which had become improved since the 1950s. Many Peacock ties were made of thick fabrics that feel heavier and fatter than older ties. Today what many people find as the epitome of an "ugly tie" is also a sterling example of the artistic expression of the seventies. Not again until the late nineties did ties present so much color, design, and fun.

90

In 1971, Woman's Day offered patterns and directions for making knitted ties, probably inspired by the popular interest in home-made items.

Lotsa stripes in 1973!

Reis of New Haven Ties showing peacock tie in 5" width, from *Esquire*, September 1970.

Diagonal Stripes - Marked Polyester, dry clean only, RN 42961; Brittania 100% imported Polyester, WPL 2555; Polyester tie marked Damon.

Peacock ties circa 1971.

Countess Mara ties from 1972. In later years, the Countess Mara lines have featured simpler, more conservative ties.

Below:
Diagonal Stripes - Brown, gold and pink stripe Polyester tie, RN 45590; Brittania "Fashion Craft" in 45% Dacron Polyester / 55% silk, WPL 2555; tie in gold and brown tones marked Ernst of San Francisco, 50% wool / 50% Dacron Polyester, RN 22681.

Diagonal Stripes -
Marked all polyester by
the Custom Cravateer;
marked BJE Ernst, 100%
Trevira Polyester; marked
Wemblon by Wembley.

Diagonal Stripes -
Three polyester ties.
The middle tie is
marked Wemblon
Fabric by Wembley.

"Next time you feel groovy, wear a tie that expresses all that. Sass out the world in a new five-incher." - from an ad for Liebert Cravats in Gentleman's Quarterly 1970

"The neckwear industry, victor in its battle a couple of years ago against the threat of turtlenecks, is now enjoying its best year, with wider widths and new fibers said to be responsible for much of the upsurge." - from the New York Times, November 1969

"Suddenly male neckwear has taken off in a surprising direction - on the wings of the "butterfly" bow tie. Polka dots, stripes and plaids with 3 inch spans are sprouting from under men's chins all over the landscape. It's part of the "layered" look, a mannered ensemble of bow tie, sleeveless sweater-vest, pleated pants and sports jacket that any 1940s fan of Archie Andrews would instantly recognize. But the new bows come 3 times the size of Archie's comic book version and are perched on the adams apple of men old enough to be his grandfather. Another lapse into nostalgia? 'Just more of the male peacock,' sighs a spokesman for Neiman-Marcus in Dallas." - from Newsweek, January 1973

Diagonal Stripes - Marked Wembley; marked Towncraft by Penney, 100% double knit Polyester; marked Liebert.

Above:
Diagonal Stripes - 100% Polyester tie by Wembley, WPL 4075; marked Foreman & Clark 100% Polyester, RN 22356.

Diagonal Stripes - Floral and paisley tie marked Par Excellence; 100% Polyester tie marked Trevira; marked 100% Trevira Polyester by BJE Ernst, RN 22681; marked 100% imported Polyester by Fashion Craft, WPL 2555.

Diagonal Stripes - Bottom to top: 65% Acetate 35% Rayon, RN 34888; marked 100% Acetate, RN 43170; marked Rhodes, 100% Polyester, WPL 2555.

Diagonal Stripes - Marked Gino Pompeii, hand woven in Italy of terytal textured Polyester, RN 43170; marked designed in Italy by Angelo Correlli; marked Air Lene.

Diagonal Stripes - Marked Mr. John, Beau Brummell, all Polyester, WPL 124; marked Brittania 100% Polyester.

Diagonal Stripes - Marked del soldato, Meier & Frank, imported all silk, RN 17843, weighted up to 40%; unmarked; marked all Polyester WPL 124.

Diagonal Stripes - Marked Wemblon fabric by Wembley; marked California Classics; marked Ernst, San Francisco, 100% Polyester, RN 22681.

"Last week the women's page of the London Daily Mirror ran a feature article on more women wearing men's fashions. The magazine article concluded by instructing the fashion-liberated women in a new talent they will need to learn: the art of tying a four-in-hand tie." - from Vogue, April 1972

Diagonal Stripes - Marked Resilio; marked all Polyester by Monsieur Cravateur, WPL 10580; marked Dessin Pierre.

Diagonal Stripes - Left marked par excellence, Towncraft by Penney's, 100% double knit Polyester; right marked All polyester by Custom Cravateers, WPL 10590.

Diagonal Stripes - 100% Dacron Polyester tie marked Fashion Craft, WPL 2555; Marked A. Sulka & Company, all silk; 100% imported acetate tie marked Cornell California, RN 20360.

Diagonal Stripes - Marked John Blair, 100% Dacron Polyester, RN 23003; marked 100% Acetate, RN 22047.

Diagonal Stripes - Top marked Wemblon fabric by Wembley; bottom marked Reis of New Haven, all Polyester.

Left:
Diagonal Stripes - 100% Polyester marked Kupper, Berkeley Cravats Ltd., Woven in France, RN 30187; marked Brittania, 100% imported Polyester, WPL 2555; unmarked tie with floral design.

Below:
Diagonal Stripes - Golden colored tie marked Colloseo Roma, imported from Italy, 100% Acetate, RN 43170; marked Brittania, 100% Polyester; marked Brittania, 100% Polyester.

Paisley - Blue and silver tie marked 65% Acetate / 35% Rayon, RN 33585; brown tie marked 100% Polyester, WPL 4075; gold/orange tie marked Brittania, 100% Polyester, WPL 2555.

Paisley - Marked Grenada by Excello, 100% Polyester; marked Brittania, 100% imported Polyester, WPL 2555; marked Ties Plus, 100% Dacron Polyester.

Paisley - 100% polyester tie marked Caslon by Castle; 100% imported polyester tie marked Brittania; marked Wembley, 100% Polyester.

Paisley - Orange/gold tie marked
Designed in Italy by Angelo Correlli, made
of imported Polyester fabric, RN 15500;
orange and blue tie marked Brittania.

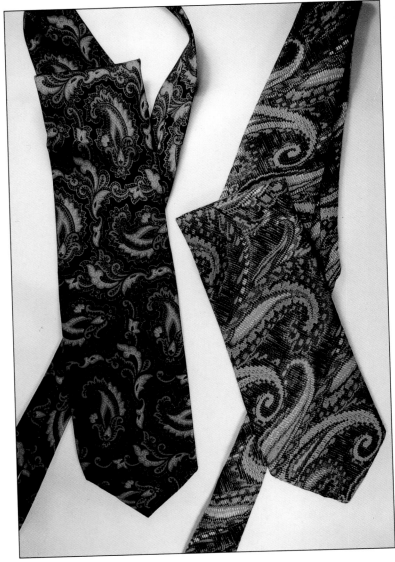

"Personally, I like the wider ties with the bigger knots that are being worn today; they're bright and colorful, and offer you a wonderful opportunity for self-expression. They also offer you a much wider area on which to spill things, if you're so inclined." - O. E. Schoeffler, Fashion Advisor to Esquire, from April 1971

Paisley - Lush paisley tie marked The
Fashion Post; marked Brittania, made
of imported Polyester, WPL 2555.

Allover design - Marked
Designed by Hardy Amies
London, 100% Polyester;
marked Grenada by Excello,
100% imported Polyester,
WPL 1887.

Allover design - Red, white and blue tie
marked 100% nylon Gabardine by Sherman.
Top marked 100% imported Rhodia Acetate.

Allover design - Marked Wemblon fabric by Wembley; op art tie
marked 100% Dacron Polyester; unmarked tie with zodiac signs.

Above:
Allover design - Marked
Pierre Cardin, imported
Polyester; marked Towncraft
Plus by Penney's, 100%
Polyester, RN 43804; red tie
marked Brittania.

Allover design - racing
flags marked Montgomery
Wards 100% Polyester, RN
15901; woven plaid
unmarked; tie with playing
card design marked 100%
Polyester, RN 17595.

Allover design - Discs and diagonals design marked Wembely; allover lines marked Simon's, Made in Italy of 100% silk; unmarked tie with white balls.

Allover design - Three unmarked ties with graphic designs. The op-art tie in the middle has a design reminiscent of artist M. C. Escher's work.

Allover design -Marked Imported all silk, RN 15500; marked Riviera 100% Polyester, WPL 1687; marked Le Chevron, RN 27326, 100% Terytal Polyester, Loomed in Italy.

Allover design - Marked imported 100% Acetate, Italian Rhodia; right unmarked tie in red and white.

Allover design - green and brown grid tie marked 100% French Rhodia, RN 28928; Tie of many squares marked 100% Acetate, RN 34888.

Allover design - Marked The Gay Blade; right marked Castle, 100% Polyester (original price tag $3.00).

Wild and Weird - Three bold graphics ties that are unmarked.

Allover design - Marked Towncraft par Excellence by Penney's; iridescent tie marked imported Rhodia, all Acetate; iridescent green tie marked Wemblon by Wembley, 100% Polyester; marked Towncraft par Excellence by Penney.

Wild and Weird - Three wild ties that are, unfortunately, unmarked. The tie on the left feels like cotton and the other two are definitely Polyester.

Wild and Weird - Two beauties of 1970s vintage. The tie on the left is marked Imported Textured Polyester, RN 16861. The tie on the right in hot pink, smiley face yellow and white is unmarked.

Wild and Weird - Marked Penney's Towncraft; unmarked red-orange tie.

Wild and Weird - Swirl patterns on left by Liebert and on right, Wemblon fabric by Wembley.

"Its seems that at least once a season, some fashion pundit makes a statement striking a blow for masculine "freedom," predicting that men will no longer put up with the tyranny of the tie. But today, after all those predictions, ties are more popular than ever before. The reason couldn't be simpler; the explosion of pattern, fabric and color, coupled with a bigger expanse on which to exhibit them, has made the ties of the last few years nothing short of sensational." - O. E. Schoeffler, Fashion Advisor to Esquire, from September 1971

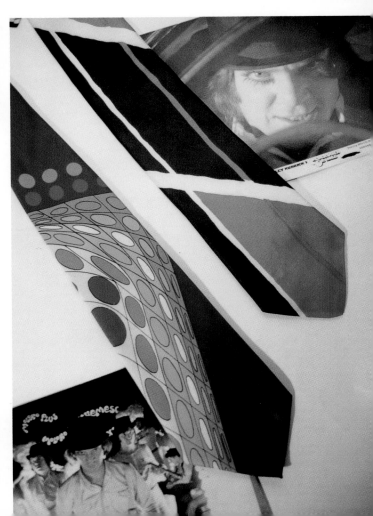

Wild and Weird - Ties with very bold graphics include on left, Designed in Italy by Angelo Correlli of 100% Polyester, RN 15500; and on right, marked Vapre, all Tricel Triacetate fabric from England, RN 20652.

Wild and Weird - Brown tie with figures crossing bridges marked Adrian, textured Polyester, RN 16861; green tie with bucolic setting marked 100% Polyester, RN 30797.

Wild and Weird - Unmarked; marked Wemblon by Wembley.

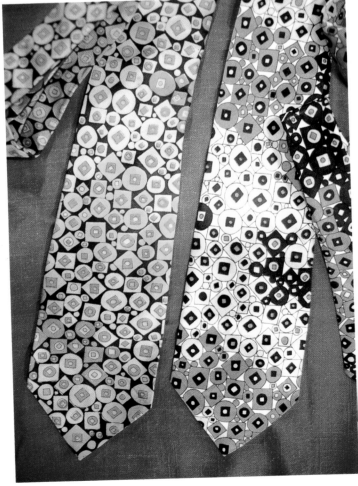

Wild and Weird Designs - Two ties with circle and square allover designs by Prince Consort. Both have clips on the back for attaching to your shirt.

Wild and Weird - Farm pattern marked "Qiana" 100% Nylon, RN 34888.

Above:
Wild and Weird - The images on the tie on the left seem to be a parody of the painting by artist Andrew Wyeth titled "Christina's World." The design on the tie shows Christina, after selling the "farm," depicted lolling on a penthouse balcony in luxury at the bottom of the tie. Very Weird!marked Uncommon Threads by John Henry;
Right tie "By the Bay" marked Berkeley Cravats, the European Look.

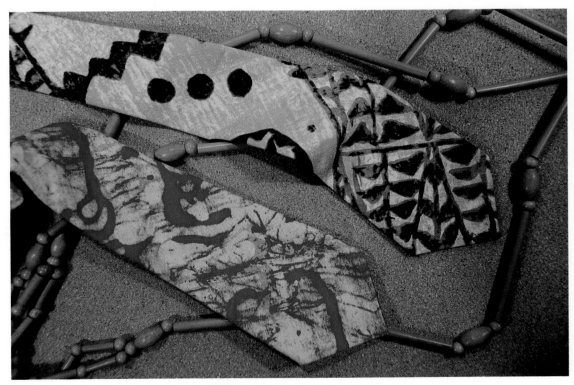

Earth tones - Both marked Kanaka Ties, 100% Cotton, Made in Hawaii.

Earth tones - Bottom, unmarked; Top, marked Via Veneto, 100% Polyester, RN 23003 (separate tag reads 100% Polyester RN 34888).

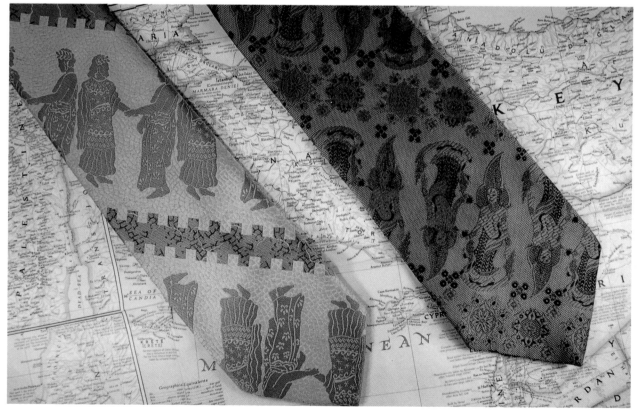

Earth tones - Greek figures adorn the left tie marked Designed in Italy by Angelo Correlli; Thai dancers on blue ground marked Wemblon fabric by Wembley.

Earth tones - A denim and floral tie and a
plain brown tie with stitching, both unmarked.

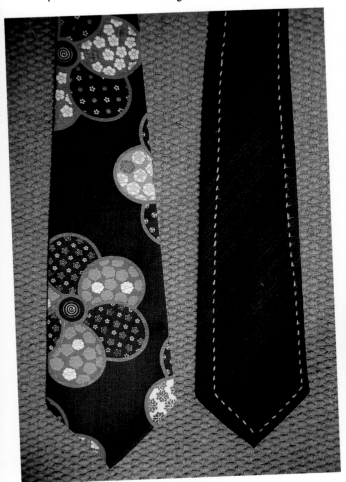

Earth tones - Three ties in rich earth tones with geometric designs
marked respectively, , Brittania, Wembley and Custom Cravateer.

Three ties with Classic designs. Greek frieze and griffins, unmarked; all silk
tie marked Cantini 1923 Firenze; Egyptian frieze design by Schiaparelli.

Four Polyester ties. The bottom left is marked Brittania Qiana Plus and the bottom right tie is marked 100% Dacron Polyester by Superba.

Top left unmarked; bottom left marked 100% Acetate Woven in France; top right marked Wemblon Fabric by Wembley; bottom right tie has Happy Fathers Day! handpainted on back.

Bold stripes marked
100% Dacron
Polyester, RN 34888;
geometric design
marked 100%
International Polyester.

Marked All silk made in Scotland; marked "Scarborough Fair"
100% Polyester; marked Express 100% silk.

Five clip-on ties marked, from , J. C. Penney; Penney's Towncraft Redi-Snap; Beau Brummell Snapper; Wemblon Fabric by Wembley.

"The tie, or more classically, the necktie, has had earth flung on its coffin time and time again by fashion pundits. It's always just about to disappear in favor of ergonomically designed shirt collars, but instead changes to mesh with the mood and requirements of the fashion times." - from the Sunday Oregonian, March 1971

Right:
Clip-on ties all marked Snapper except third from left marked the Treasury WPL 11935.

Below Left:
Left marked 100% Acetate by Mitzi Cravat, WPL 10580; right marked 100% Polyester, RN 16484.

Below Right:
Three Polyester ties, the middle one with the leaping deer is marked Adrian.

8. Eigh-ties & Beyond

By the mid- to late 1970s, the tie industry experienced a slow-down. Conservatism returned to America and was reflected in the clothing fashions of the 1980s. Ties became gradually thinner to more traditional proportions and they were made with more restrained and respectable designs. Many Americans yearned for traditional values after two decades of upheaval. By the mid-1980s, three trends appeared to re-awaken the style of ties:

Designer ties - "The time was ripe for a new kind of tie, one that would convey wealth, status, security and a familiarity with the worlds of glamour and privilege which seemed to be closed to the mass of men once more. And the big name designers were ready to provide it. The "designer tie" - one, in the modern sense, that has not necessarily come from the studio of a famous fashion designer, but which has been approved by the star and prominently carries his or her trademark, name or initials - was perfect for its era. Men were eager to buy the positive image associated with the designer name, women loved the link to glamour and luxury, and the designers themselves wanted to make money that couture was no longer generating. The licensing concept has now revolutionized high fashion, turning men and women who were once dressmakers into society figures and billionaires who endorse everything from

orange juice to car rugs." Sarah Gibbings, *The Tie: Trends and Traditions*

Retro ties - The first ties made to look like ties of an earlier era appeared in the later 1960s, as part of the first waves of the Nostalgia Craze. Through the 1970s, interest in retro ties waned, but by the mid-1980s the Retro Look was appearing frequently in a much better attempt to recreate the Bold Look. Most popular were bold, geometric, up-dated Art Deco patterns. Marketers found that retro ties appealed to women. Also popular were animal and floral motifs, paisleys, and overall geometrics.

Power ties - Though initially conservative design-wise, new ties were presented as able to express something of a man's personality (if not his individuality). *Esquire Magazine* noted in 1987, "Ask if ties tell anything about the man who wears them, and men tell us that for the vast middle class it doesn't mean a thing. But if a man has read *The Power Look* by Egon von Furstenberg, he's conscious of his total clothing message and his tie is part of the package." Von Furstenberg's 1978 book, along with John Molloy's book *Dress for Success*, was a highly influential manual of style, purporting ties (preferably by designers) as symbols of power and success. The first half of the 1980s was the era of the Power Tie.

Wemco's Belgravia line of silk ties from MR Magazine, 1996.

"We, being the mothers and fathers of that child, the tie, don't feel that there is any such item as an ugly tie," declared Gerald Andersen, executive Director of the Neckwear Association. "We believe there is an out-of-date tie, an out-of-style tie and even an out-of-sorts tie. Referring to someone's tie as ugly could create self consciousness. But over all, it generates interest in ties."
- from The New York Times, June 1987

Introducing Burton Morris
CONTEMPORARY ARTIST • ILLUSTRATOR

Burton Morris designer ties by Zanzara from MR Magazine, 1996.

"Common Spirit" ties, a division of MMG Corporation, neckwearcreated from original artwork and editorial from ® Hallmark Cards, Inc. ® Hallmark Licensing, Inc. from MR Magazine, 1996.

The problem with dictating a single color tie as preferable, no matter how power-laden, is that all the power hungry men wind up wearing the same color tie. Eventually there is a revolt and a search for a new color or different designs. And that's what actually happened. The first Power tie was yellow, but by the late 1980s no one could agree on what the Power color was. For a while red was considered *the* new Power color, but various shops around the country reported selling teal, burgundy, wine or pink colored ties as Power ties. Then Power tie variations appeared as The Retro Power Tie, The Paisley Power Tie, The Jazzy Tie, and the Gutsy Tie. Some claimed there was no single Power tie but a Power Look; some predicted the Power tie was on the wane, and still others said the days of the Power tie were already over. The stock market plunge of October, 1987, is pointed to as a turning point in men's fashions, as it was the antithesis of all that the Power Look stood for.

Contemporary designers gave ties prestige in the 1980s by placing their own emblems on the fronts of the ties they designed. From top left: Xandrin, Oleg Cassini, and John Wertz; bottom left: Pierre Cardin and Geoffrey Beene.

Above:
Unmarked allover design; dapper gentlemen design marked Woven in Italy; marked Elaan.

Polyester tie marked BBB New York City, a dead ringer for a Fifties skinny tie; two silk ties marked Made in Italy.

From the left: marked Don Loper of California, 100% Polyester; paisleys marked Nordstrom, made in Italy; leaf forms design by Countess Mara; marked Enro Casuals.

Marked JB Herringbone 100% Rayon; marked Gino Pompeii 100% silk; marked Elaan; allover design marked Gino Pompeii 100% silk; marked Elaan.

Allover blue tie marked Blazer; marked Leatherback Satins by Wembley; allover design red tie marked Britches of Georgetown; marked Leatherback Satins by Wembley.

Blue floral marked TJW by Mervyn's; leaf design marked John Weitz; marked TJW by Mervyn's.

Three floral prints: left marked Rooster all cotton; center and right marked Allyn St. George, WPL 4075.

Bright floral tie marked Tango by Max Raab; "Salad" tie marked Uniforms for You, 100% Polyester.

Four ties displaying a style reminiscent of the Bold Look. : marked Retro Design Studios; red polyester tie marked Don Loper, Beverly Hills; allover bold pattern marked Pierre Balmain; abstract design marked Chez Roffe, New York, RN 77816.

Golfing Santas on Polyester
tie by Cape Cod; skiers on
100% red silk tie; cotton
bolls design by Resilio.

Below:
Geese hunters design on unmarked tie; yellow tie marked Don
Loper, Beverly Hills; mice design on red tie marked Brooks
Brothers, 65% silk / 35% polyester, woven in England.

Five ties with Bold Look-inspired designs: all silk marked Bill Blass; 100% silk marked Swing; all silk by Bill Blass; all silk muted print by Aldolfo; marked Miles Davis.

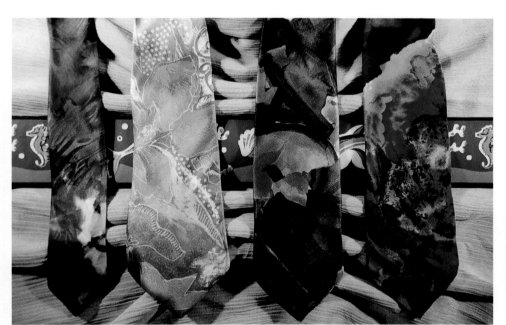

Four ties with muted designs. : narrow tie marked all Polyester by Policy; peach and blue tie marked Windridge by Mervyn's; marked Surrey Sophisticates, 100% Polyester; marked John Henry, 100% silk crepe.

Imported silk tie with paisley motifs marked TKS for Nordstrum, RN 22356; bold silk tie marked Made in Italy; allover design marked Geoffry Beene; silk tie marked Facets, RN 88335.

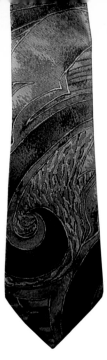

These ties have their own "Bold Look" that says NOW. : muted design on polyester tie marked Christian Pelini, RN 20797; giant paisley design marked John Wertz; colorful circles on tie marked Duomo Milano, High Fashion; silk tie with blue, red and gray swirls marked Oleg Cassini, Made in China, RN 43170.

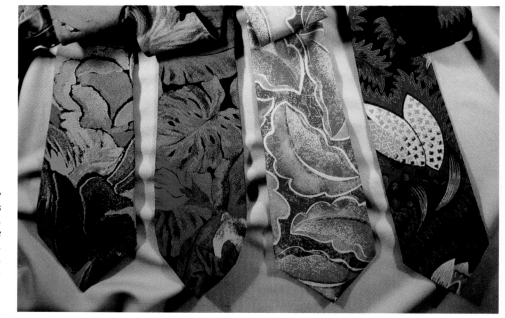

These four ties display designs in earth tones popular in the 1990s. The two at the left are marked Jonathan; next, marked Swing; last, marked Railroad.

All silk tie with Hotel Monte Carlo signs marked Harvard Fine Neckwear; contemporary paisleys on silk marked Rooster, RN 57962; ski posters design marked Concerto; all silk tie with pepper dancer design by Tabasco, WPL 4075.

"Reporters in Las Vegas for the Fashion Association's Best of Spring 1996 show got a glimpse of what's ahead for men's tie. The Look: Casual. Ties that represent the soul of a man whose wearing it. Ties dancing with Harley-Davidson motorcycles, sassy bottles of Tabasco sauce and Elvis Presley's pouty mug. Who's wearing it: All kinds of men. The so-called casual Friday look is in - which means that the red-power tie's red-hot days are smoke. Odds of seeing it next season: Pretty good. The trend towards casual dress has yet to crest."
-Michelle Trappen for the Oregonian 1996

From the 1990s: marked Forte, 100% Polyester; bold design marked Carlo Palazzi, 100% Polyester; "new wave" design narrow tie marked Tie Chic by Ahna, San Francisco; marked Surrey, 100% Rayon RN 23896.

Ice hockey gear design by Nicole Miller; sun, moon and stars design marked Limited, 100% silk; computer circuit design marked Software Ltd; Trumpets design by Ralph Marlin.

Three novelty ties by Ralph Marlin: "Lone Ranger"; "Starry Night"; "Lucy and Gang".

"While Mr. Abramoff has been hawking fish neckties in Wisconsin, his rainbow trout, salmon, pike and tuna have been selling out at designer boutiques in New York, Chicago and Cape Cod. In May, Mr. Abramoff's Ralph Marlin & Company (named after a mythical charter boat fisherman from Rosa Rita, Mexico, who wore real fish around his neck for good luck) started shipping fish neckties around the country. They have sold 7,000 ties so far with orders for 20,000 more." - from the New York Times, July 1986

Two fish design ties. Top marked "Muskie"; bottom marked "Designer Tuna" by Ralph Marlin.

We appear today, at the end of the 1990s, to be experiencing another explosion of design and color in ties. What will this trend be called - the Global Look? - the Casual Look? Whatever it is called, ties of the 1990s are offsprings of the Retro and Power ties of the 1980s: free, bold, colorful, artistic, expressive and sometimes unusual. Many small and independent designers are joining well-established designers in creating a myriad of images both artistic and expressive. There are all-over patterns, reproductions of famous paintings, moody abstracts, florals, and crazy versions of Bold Look ties as well as reproductions of 1950s skinnies.

Most novel of all the new designs are the licensed character ties. Almost all time periods have characters of popular culture including famous people, animals, and cartoons, and today they are making their way onto mass-produced ties for men. In the late 1990s you can have the likes of Daffy Duck, Lucille Ball, Elvis Presley, Rush Limbaugh, The Cat in the Hat, The Beatles, Charlie Chaplin, Marilyn Monroe, The Flinstones, the Jetsons and countless other real and animated characters on ties to adorn your chest.

Based on an overview of the tie styles in the second half of the twentieth century, it is my guess that another return to more traditional styles for ties lies in the near future. In that case, it would stand to reason that the most memorable ties from contemporary times will be "re-discovered." Which ties from today will speak to the fashion dressers of the future?

9. Bow-Ties

The bowtie has suffered this subservient fate and borne it well. Despite all the fashion cycles of men's neckwear, the bowtie has always returned. Fat or skinny, solid or boldly patterned, the bowtie has provided a constant alternative in the world of men's neckwear. There are examples of bowties from each of the necktie styles: the Bold Look, novelties, skinnies, the Peacock Look (called "butterfly bows"), the Power ties, and character ties.

Spur bow ties from the *Saturday Evening Post*, December 1927.

Wembley bow ties from *Esquire*, December 1952.

Sherman Bow Ties from *Esquire*, May 1944.

Hand-tied - Left marked Inviso
bow tie; unmarked overall
design; marked Adjusto tie.

Hand-tied - Left marked
Wembley; marked Inviso
bow tie; marked Wembley.

Hand-tied - Left marked the
Original Adjusto tie; marked JT
RN 35408; marked Wembley.

Hand-tied - marked Inviso bow tie; unmarked overall design; marked Adjusto tie.

"It has been a little over a year now since tie salesmen began noticing the growing demand for bowties, but before jumping to the conclusion that Frank Sinatra started the trend, we consulted an expert for his advice. It wasn't Sinatra and it wasn't Franklin Roosevelt, even though he wore bow ties in the White House when Frankie was a teenager. It's just that the guys got tired of wearing the same old tie. That's all any style indicates - somebody decided he wanted to wear something different. When enough people decide they want a change you have a new style. So now it's bow ties." - from the New York Times August 1945

Hand-tied - marked 100% silk, RN 18236; unmarked design in blue; unmarked shield design.

Pre-tied - Top marked Beauclip;
marked Metro; marked Spiegler;
marked Ormond, NY.

Pre-tied - Top marked Evergrip; marked U-Clip;
marked Ormond; marked U-Clasp.

"For men who can't or won't tie their own bow ties, a prefabricated bow, already tied, recently appeared on the market. It is mounted on a collar clip, unlike the old jazzbow ties of the Twenties, which snapped around the neck on elastic, and slips neatly onto the shirt collar." - from the New York Times, August 1945

Pre-tied - Left
marked U-Clip;
marked Ormond;
marked Ormond;
marked Ormond;
marked Quik-klip.

Pre-tied - All
marked Ormond.

Below:
Pre-tied - Left marked Ormond; marked Everclip;
marked Metro; marked Everclip; marked Ormond.

Pre-tied - Top marked Wembley; marked Wembley; marked Ormond; marked Ormond; marked Best-Clip.

Pre-tied - Top marked Beau Clip; marked Ever-Grip; marked Ormond; marked Wembley.

Pre-tied - Top marked Ever-grip; marked Ormond; marked Wembley; marked Best-Clip.

Pre-tied - Boy's bowties and a string tie marked Royal.

"If you wear a bow-tie you will not be taken seriously. But if you are of strong character, then a bow-tie could well come in handy to soften the image. However, otherwise, with a bow-tie around your neck, you will not be considered responsible people. Nobody will entrust you with important business." - from The Book of Ties

Pre-tied - Felt Christmas bowties, both marked Ormond on metal clip.

Pre-tied- All by Ormond.

Pre-tied - In the 1970s, bowties were big and showy.

10. Tie Related Beau-ties

Items related to ties are interesting to a tie collector for they, too, reflect the culture in which they were created. Among the most interesting are tie mock-ups which were used by tie salesmen as samples of the artwork available. They are printed on cardboard that is shaped like a tie.

It is surprising, but true, that old tie racks are hard to find. In the recent past, when interest in collectible ties was beginning, one found a lot of pressed wood tie racks from the 1930s and 1940s with molded horse heads, ships, and hunting scenes. Now they appear to be scarce. Home-made tie racks, in a variety of materials, were a favorite project for hobbyists and boy scouts alike. Magazines of days past have advertisments for commercially made racks that folded, gripped or rotated! Where are they all?

Tie display - Circa 1930s, carved wooden hand, about 36" high.

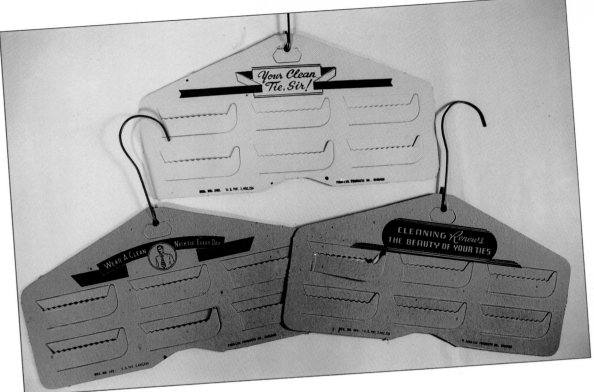

Your Clean Tie, Sir!

WEAR A CLEAN Necktie Every Day

CLEANING *Renews* THE BEAUTY OF YOUR TIES

Above:
Paper - Cardboard tie hangers with snappy slogans marked Paralux Prods. Co. Chicago given out by dry cleaners with cleaned ties, circa 1950.

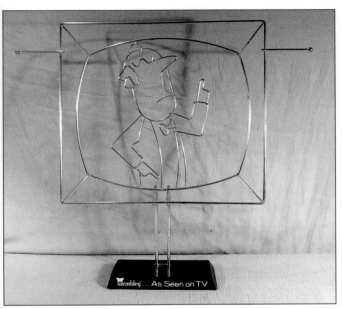

Wembley ... As Seen on TV

Tie display - for Wembley ties, metal with wooden base inscribed Wembley - As Seen on TV.

Your NECKTIES DRY CLEANED AND FINISHED TO LOOK NEW AGAIN.

Paper - The front of a paper protector for a wire coat hanger from a dry cleaner advertising their tie cleaning service, circa 1940s or 1950s.

Tie mock-ups - The same bird design in two different color schemes.

Paper - Simplicity pattern #9400 for home sewing ties, circa 1970.

Tie press - "Little Valet" electric tie press by Perfection Mfg. Co., Los Angeles, California. Patent # issued February 1934. The instructions read, "Slip flat side of press between the lining and front of tie so far as it will go. Moisten tie with damp cloth and the tie will steam back to original shape and appearance."

Tie mock-ups - Fantasy women: tropical goddess, Scheherezade belly dancer; woman caught in a spider's web (Weird!).

Tie mock-ups - Maple leaves, poppies, and oak leaves designs.

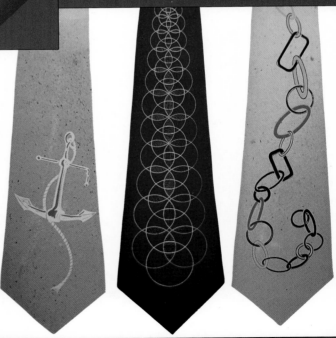

Tie mock-ups - Anchor, circles, and chains designs.

Tie mock-ups - Calf roping, fox hunting, and horse designs.

Tie mock-ups - Butterflies, fishing motif, and cherries designs.

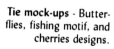

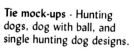

Tie mock-ups - Hunting dogs, dog with ball, and single hunting dog designs.

Tie mock-ups - Saddle horse, bucking bronco, and Lippizanner horse designs.

Tie mock-ups - Three cowboy rodeo event designs.

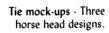

Tie mock-ups - Three horse head designs.

Tie Rack - Wood with wood veneer and metal, marked Nu-Dell Manufacturing Company Chicago, copyright 1939. The little windows are a "style chart" which shows the proper color coordination of shirt, tie and suit; the chart is changed by turning the dial.

A TIE'S BEST FRIEND!

Beautiful ties individually held by colorful Red, Ivory, Green and Blue flexible plastic holders on a Sparkling Clear Lucite Rack makes your wardrobe door glow like a Rembrandt painting.

TIES CAN'T WRINKLE OR FALL OFF. Each tie kept neat —orderly—easily selected at a glance.

TI-D-TIE RACK is an Ideal gift — sturdily built to give years of every day service. Smartly boxed. Money back guarantee. No C.O.D.'s Please.

XMAS GIVING MADE EASY. Send list of names and addresses with order. We will enclose gift cards with racks, mark packages "Do not open until Xmas" & mail for early Xmas delivery. **ORDER NOW.**

DeLuxe Lucite Rack 18½" long, 48 holders
$5.00 postpaid
DeLuxe Lucite Rack 10½" long, 24 holders
$3.00 postpaid
Steel Rack 10½" long with baked enamel ivory wrinkle finish, 24 holders,
$1.75 each, 3 for **$5.00** postpaid
U. S. Patent No. 2403834

FRED H. STREIT CO. 100 W. Chicago Ave. Chicago 10, Illinois

Tie rack - TI-D-TIE RACK advertised in *Esquire*, December 1947.

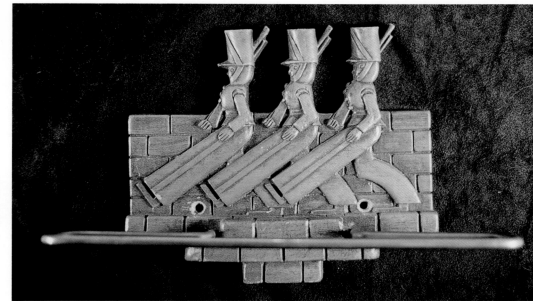

Tie Rack - Wood composition and metal featuring marching toy soldiers, marked Sirocco Wood.

Tie Rack - Wood with burned teepee design, a souvenir of La Grande, Ore.

Tie Rack - Wood composition and metal featuring a military airfield with The Pioneer airplane.

Tie Rack - Snap-Rack advertised in *Esquire*, December 1947.

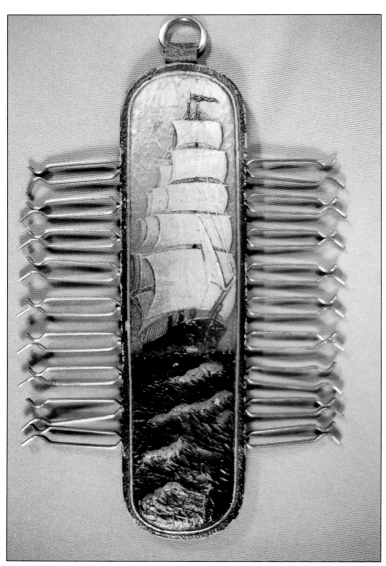

Tie Rack - tooled and painted leather with metal; the patent number on the back corresponds to the year 1933.

Tie Rack - Wood and enamel paint with five pegs at the bottoms of the letters.

Bibliography

Chaille, Francois. *The Book of Ties*. New York & Paris; Flammarion, 1994.

Connike, Yvonne. *Fashions of a Decade -The 1960s*. New York; Facts on File, 1990.

de Marly, Diana. *Fashions for Men, An Illustrated History*. New York; Holmes & Meier Publishers, Inc., 1986.

Dyer, Rod and Ron Spark. *Fit To Be Tied: Vintage Ties of the Forties and Early Fifties*. New York; Abbeville Press, 1987.

Esquire magazine. 1944, 1947-1949, 1952, 1970, 1976.

Gibbings, Sarah. *The Tie: Trends and Traditions*. London; Studio Editions Ltd., 1990.

Good Housekeeping magazine. 1950-1952, 1954, 1957, 1959.

Gross, Kim Johnson and Jeff Stone. *Chic Simple, Shirt and Tie*. New York; Alfred Knopf, 1993.

Holiday magazine. 1947.

Holland, Saddler, and Langford. *Textiles*. New York; The McMillan Co. Inc., 1979.

Jerde, Judith. *Encyclopedia of Textiles*. New York; Facts on File, 1992.

LaBarre, Kathleen & Kate. *Reference Book of Men's Vintage Clothing*. Portland; LaBarre Books, 1992.

Life magazine. 1942.

Man-Made Fiber and Textile Dictionary. The Celanese Corp, 1975.

Montgomery Ward catalog. Fall/winter 1945.

MR Neckwear Handbook 1996. New York; MR Magazine, 1996.

Neese, Michael & Shelle. *Cowboy Ties*. Layton, Utah; Peregrine Smith Books, 1994.

Redbook magazine. 1950.

Saturday Evening Post magazine. 1927, 1946, 1951.

The Story of Rayon. New York; The Viscose Company, 1937.

West magazine. 1945.

Pricing

I agree with the detractors of price guides - the prices are arbitrary. And that's just the point. This allows room for people to take in all considerations and negotiate. Read the following carefully. The prices in this book are based on:

Condition - The prices listed in this book are for ties in VERY GOOD to EXCELLENT condition (even if the tie shown is not.) Stained ties will lower the price by 1/3 or 1/2. Torn or dismembered ties are worth relatively little.

Supply and Demand - a renewed interest in a certain era or style of tie will raise prices as demand increases. Supplies are based on what is available location-wise.

Location - The prices ranges in this book are meant to accommodate the variance of prices nationwide, including urban and rural areas. The prices listed in this book reflect the price you would pay in a vintage clothing store and, on the low end, the price at a thrift store or estate sale.

Observation - Prices seen on both East and West coasts in vintage clothing outlets, estate sales and thrift stores helped to determine the values in this book.

3. For-ties Bold

The Bold Look continues to be popular as it slowly passes into antique status. There is still much available, but the days of the 2 for a dollar are long gone.
Plain or not-so-interesting design or pattern - $6-15
Highly desired or unusual design or pattern - $15-30

For-ties Designer
Loper - $12-25
Mara or Lesser - $20-60
Dali - $300-500
Oriental silks - $15-30

4. Novel-ties
Special-ties - $10-25
Girlie - $20-50
"Peek-a-boo" - $75-100
Hand-painted - $25-75

5. Fif-ties Skinnies and more

These period ties are seeing a surge in popularity. The skinny "cocktail lounge" era ties associated with Frank Sinatra, jazz combos and Las Vegas are popular with the younger generation. Pop, Op, and Mod ties are extremely hard to locate.
Standard width - Plain or not-so-interesting design or pattern - $6-15
Standard width - Highly desired or unusual design or pattern - $15-30
Skinny ties, plain - $5-15
Skinny ties, fancy - $12-20
Op, Pop or Mod or Psychedelic ties - $20-50

7. Seven-ties Peacock

When someone enters an ugly tie contest, they usually pick a 1970s tie. This should tell you something right there - what's out will soon be in! Now is a good time to collect this era as supply is great and demand is low. These ties are readily available at thrift stores, garage sales, and anyplace people are getting ready to throw away everything.
Plain or not-so-interesting design or pattern - $5-10
Highly desired or unusual design or pattern - $10-20

9. Bow-ties
All eras, hand-tied and clip-ons - $5-10

10. Tie Related Beau-ties
Paper ephemera - $5-15
Tie press - $10-20
Mock-ups - $10-20 each
Tie racks - $5-25